WESTERN SERIES AND SEQUELS

GARLAND REFERENCE LIBRARY
OF THE HUMANITIES
(VOL. 625)

GARLAND BIBLIOGRAPHIES ON SERIES AND SEQUELS

Science Fiction and Fantasy
Series and Sequels
A Bibliography
Volume 1: Books
compiled by
Tim Cottrill
Martin H. Greenberg
Charles G. Waugh

Science Fiction and Fantasy
Series and Sequels
Volume 2: Articles
compiled by
Tim Cottrill
Martin H. Greenberg
Charles G. Waugh

Western Series and Sequels
A Reference Guide
compiled by
Bernard A. Drew
with Martin H. Greenberg
and Charles G. Waugh

Mystery Series and Sequels
compiled by
Frank D. McSherry
Francis Nevins, Jr.
Charles G. Waugh
Martin H. Greenberg

WESTERN SERIES AND SEQUELS
A Reference Guide

Bernard A. Drew
with Martin H. Greenberg
and Charles G. Waugh

GARLAND PUBLISHING, INC. · NEW YORK & LONDON
1986

Library of Congress Cataloging-in-Publication Data
Drew, Bernard A. (Bernard Alger), 1950–
Western series and sequels.

(Garland bibliographies on series and sequels)
(Garland reference library of the humanities ;
vol. 625)
Includes index.
1. Western stories—Bibliography. 2. American
fiction—West (U.S.)—Bibliography. 3. Sequels
(Literature)—Bibliography. 4. Monographic series—
Bibliography. 5. West (U.S.) in literature—
Bibliography. I. Greenberg, Martin Harry. II. Waugh,
Charles. III. Title. IV. Series. V. Series: Garland
reference library of the humanities ; v. 625.
Z1251.W5D74 1986 [PS374.W4] 016.813'0874 85-45132
ISBN 0-8240-8657-0 (alk. paper)

Cover design by Alison Lew

Printed on acid-free, 250-year-life paper
Manufactured in the United States of America

CONTENTS

Buck In The Saddle Again

By Bernard A. Drew

The tall-in-the-saddle literary cowboy of yesteryear, skillful with cattle, gentle with his horse, expert with sixguns, shy with women and stern with villains, has changed.

Today as he appears in popular paperback series books, he's likely as not to be sullen or vicious, kill for pleasure, rob for a living and fork his leg over a willing woman more often than a champing horse. Yup, the American cowboy myth has definitely changed.

Fictional cowboys have long enjoyed a loyal readership. "One of the canniest paperback editors working today once told me that his company occasionally lost money on some titles in every category — except the Western," said Dean R. Koontz in *Writing Popular Fiction*. "No Western has ever lost them a dime. No enormous profit, you understand. Just modest but steady sales."

Despite their proven popularity with readers, Westerns have seldom received critical attention. For every Zane Grey, Max Brand or Louis L'Amour who might draw a rare glance from reviewers, there are a hundred Western fiction writers working in obscurity.

And the paperback series hero — disparaged even by many "serious" Western writers — ranks low in the sagebrush. This despite the fact that series cowboys now account for more than half of the Western paper-

NEW BUFFALO BILL WEEKLY (Street & Smith March 7, 1914) was typical of the turn-of-the-century dime novels. Many were later reprinted in paperback.

Jim Hatfield's exploits appeared monthly in the pulp magazine TEXAS RANGERS (Thrilling October 1942) and were reprinted in paperback.

back market. (There is no significant Western hardcover market in the 1980s.)

This bibliography of some 3,500 series titles is intended as a resource for future critical examination of the genre. The evolution of the series cowboy may be traced from his origins in mainstream literature into dime novels and pulp magazines up through the monthly-issued Longarm and Slocum books of this decade.

A number of better known writers of Western fiction are missing. Ernest Haycox, Charles Alden Seltzer, Dorothy M. Johnson, Frank Bonham and others have preferred the creative freedom of writing free-standing tales. In fact, except for job security, the appeal of series characters is perhaps stronger with readers than writers. Once a reader discovers a character he or she likes, there's an inclination to buy more of the same.

The writer, on the other hand, is somewhat limited in what he can do with his character; he has to stick close to formula, can't marry his hero off or kill him.

James Fenimore Cooper created the Western series in his Leatherstocking Tales beginning with *The Pioneer* in 1823. The Hawkeye stories "paved the way for many fictional treatments of the West which strongly resembled his patterns of plot, character and theme..." wrote John G. Cawelti in *The Six-Gun Mystique.*

"In the later 19th century, the Western formula continued to flourish in the dime novel..." he said. "Gradually the cowboy replaced the frontier scout as the archetypal Western hero. Finally in a number of works published around the turn of the century, the most important of which was Owen Wister's *The Virginian,* the Western formula arrived at most of the characteristics it has held through innumerable novels, stories, films and TV shows in the 20th century."

The wild West of 1865 to 1900 was rich in raw material. There were skirmishes between settlers and Indians reluctant to give up their lands. Law and order was haphazard. There were natural resources to be exploited. There were fertile grazing grounds to be fought over. There were railroad tracks to be laid, cities to be built. There was opportunity for power, and for corruption. The outlaw flourished. Peacekeepers

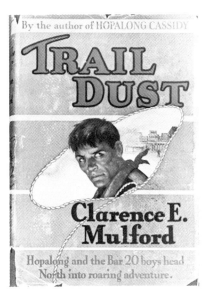 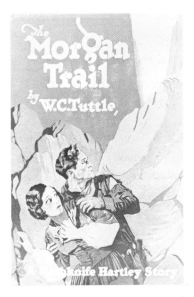

Earlier in the century, there was a major American market for hardcover Westerns such as Clarence E. Mulford's TRAIL DUST (Doubleday, Doran 1934).

W.C. Tuttle's THE MORGAN TRAIL, published in hardcover by Houghton-Mifflin in 1928, was re-issued in a less expensive hardcover edition by Grosset & Dunlap.

were kept busy. Ranchers and capitalists carved out their empires.

The literary form which grew from this wild West had already become a stereotype by the beginning of the era. Inexpensive dime novels exaggerating the Western theme were published by Beadle and Adams and read voraciously by soldiers during the Civil War.

In this century, the physical form of the formula Western has changed, but not the substance. Westerns have been published in inexpensive hardcovers, in pulpwood paper magazines and now in paperbound books — all for the popular market.

Western writer Frank Gruber in his autobiography *The Pulp Jungle* outlined seven basic Western plots: The railroad story; the ranch story; the empire story; the revenge story; the Indian and cavalry story; the outlaw story; and the marshal story.

"These seven basic Western plots are quite enough," he said. "It is not the plot that is important, it is what you do with the characters, the incidental material, the conflicts, the emotions that are plumbed."

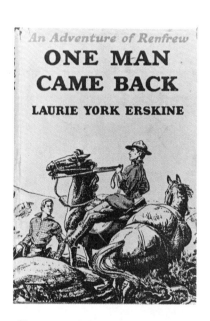
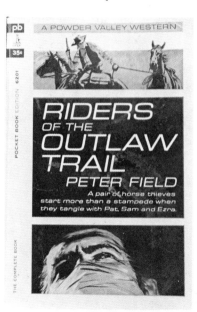

Numerous boys' and girls' book series were set in the West, or in the case of Laurie York Erskine's ONE MAN CAME BACK (D. Appleton-Century 1939), the Canadian Northwest.

Peter Field's adventures of Pat Stevens, Sam Sloan and Ezra were an early, long-running series. Shown is RIDERS OF THE OUTLAW TRAIL (Pocket 1963).

During wartime paper shortages, paperback Westerns appeared in different formats. Shown is Evan Evans' MONTANA RIDES AGAIN (Armed Services Edition).

Sequels to popular Zane Grey novels were published in the digest-size ZANE GREY WESTERN MAGAZINE (Zane Grey Western Magazine April 1970) and later collected in paperback.

Western series writers may be seen taking one of three approaches. The more "serious" ones have remained faithful to their history. Frederick Manfred, Allen W. Eckert, Louis L'Amour, Owen Rountree and Gary McCarthy are among series writers displaying research of, and affection for, their heritage. Their works are spiced with detail, and sometimes actual historical figures walk their pages.

In the middle is a solid core of formulaic writers who use the Western background as a setting for well-crafted action tales. One will find a breath of fresh air, as far as characterization and plain good writing go, in many formula Westerns. William R. Cox's Buchanan, Clifton Adams' Amos Flagg and Brian Garfield's Jeremy Six stories (all written under pseudonyms) are all highly readable.

And at the other extreme is a growing band of writers stretching the tired but willing genre in a number of mis-directions, as we will see.

Since the paperback book arrived in the 1930s, publishing houses

The British series Edge by George G. Gilman introduced a strong violent element to the Western. This is THE BLUE, THE GREY AND THE RED (New English Library 1972).

One of the longest running of all Western book series is Marshall Grover's Larry & Stretch Westerns from Australia. This is LONE STAR FIREBRANDS (Cougar no date).

have exploited every possible source for material. Cooper's works have been brought back to print. Young Wild West, Denver Dan, Buffalo Bill and others have been resurrected from the dime novels. W.C. Tuttle's Hashknife Hartley yarns have been reprinted from hardcover, as have been Blue Steele, Jim Hatfield and Rio Kid tales from the pulps.

The inexpensive pulp magazines of the 1920s and '30s, which immediately preceded the advent of paperback book publishing in the United States, were the richest source of reprint material, and anticipated most of the later trends.

Besides those characters which made the transition, there were adventurous cowboys Pistol Pete Rice and the Pecos Kid, who had their own magazines; outlaw Sonny Tabor in *Wild West Weekly*; White Eagle in *Big Chief Western*; and Senorita Scorpion in *Action Stories* — foreshadowing later hero, outlaw, Indian and female paperback series.

Many dime novel series remain unreprinted largely because their writing is greatly out of style today. The same is true of the early hardcover boys' and girls' book series. More pulp series are being revived each year primarily through the continued popularity of certain authors, such as Brand and L'Amour, who wrote prolifically for those magazines.

Walker A. Tompkins, a long-time pulp writer, explained in an article in the June 1938 *Writer's Digest*: "All branches of writing suffer from the paucity of plots, but Western stories are especially notorious for their similarity to each other. So the writer who would stand above the common herd must arrange his plots in such a way that editor and public will find them sparkling with that undefinable something called 'originality.'"

Paperback publishers, draining their reprint sources, began issuing original Western series, though there was little constructive stretching of the literary boundaries in these books. Most new series mirrored old ones in settings and plots, though as mentioned some writers infused

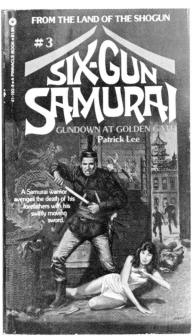

There were hundreds of formulary Westerns in the 1940s, '50s and '60s, such as Clay Randall's AMOS FLAGG HAS HIS DAY (Fawcett 1968).

Warping Western history were a number of off-beat series in the 1970s, such as Patrick Lee's Six-Gun Samurai. GUNDOWN AT GOLDEN GATE was issued by Pinnacle in 1981.

solid characterization and prose styles into their formulas.

Television, which competes with books for an audience, has influenced publishing only marginally; a handful of TV series such as "Bonanza" have prompted book series.

The movies, too, with a singular exception, have only minimally invaded the paperback series. Roy Rogers, Gene Autry and Red Ryder, popular B-Western stars of the 1940s, appeared in inexpensive juvenile books.

A rare few such as The Lone Ranger and Hopalong Cassidy conquered all media — movies, TV, radio, comic strips, hardcover and paperback books. But except for spawning a few immitators (The Masked Rider), they didn't influence the genre's direction.

The motion picture series which did leave its brand was The Man with No Name, a violent anti-hero played by Clint Eastwood in three "Spaghetti" Westerns made in the 1960s. The character drew a short series of books. But more importantly, as Jon Tuska explained in *The American West in Fiction*, writer Terry Harknett, who novelised the first entry, *A Fistful of Dollars* for a British publisher in 1967, went on to create the Edge series (as George G. Gilman) and also the Apache series with W. Laurence James (the team writing as William M. James). Both of these British Western series were picked up by an American publisher, and made an explosion. Blood and guts were in. Leading series publishers imported or commissioned their own ultra-violent cowboys, from Kilburn and Cade to Lassiter and Fargo.

This super-violence, a distinctly revisionist view of old West history, has lessened the genre's appeal for some. C.L. Sonnichsen in *From Hopalong to Hud* observed: "Western novels are indeed here today and gone tomorrow, and there are some special reasons for reader indifference. One is the feeling that we have been conned by the storytellers and scenarists who give us wrong answers about how the West was won. They have ignored the land grabbers and exploiters and played up as frontier Galahads a gang of barroom characters and part-time peace officers..."

While one might counter that the Western is, after all, simply a popular literary form and not necessarily intended to be historically accurate (any more than is the tea-room detective novel or the gothic romance), it has to be admitted that the paperback Western has gone in some crazy directions.

Since the 1970s, there have appeared Spectros, the magician cowboy; Six-Gun Samurai, the martial arts gunslinger; Klaw and Leatherhand, the disabled cowboys; Gold, the Jewish cowboy; and Breck, the born-again Christian gunfighter.

A genre already bent out of form was distorted even further in the 1980s by the second revolution which delivered the sexy cowboys. These series, termed by Tuska "merely pornography in a period setting," number more than 30. They include Foxx and Gunn, Scout and Shelter. Their bedroom (or barroom or teepee) sexual activities are usually graphic.

"Adult" Westerns actually can trace their origins to Zane Grey, who often included at least one mildly suggestive scene in each novel, and the blatantly lurid pulp titles such as *Spicy Western Stories.*

The arrival of the sexy Western also marked the beginning of a more sophisticated marketing of cowboy series. Borrowing from the romance publishers and espionage/thriller packagers, a half-dozen adult cowboy publishers have issued books on a bi-monthly or monthly schedule, distinguishing their series with bold graphic design.

The bookstore browser is thus presented with an obvious series each time he or she passes. While it took three decades for Pocket Books to bring out 87 of Peter Field's Powder Valley Westerns, more than 80 Longarm and Slocum books have been published in six years' time, and the Making of America saga series has more than 50 entries so far on its

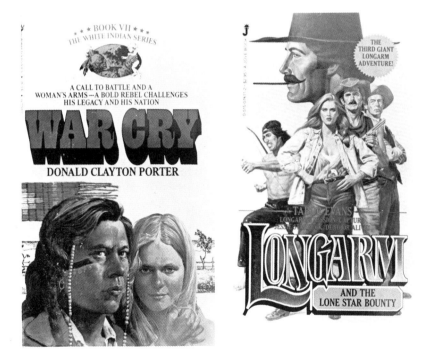

The Western saga series blended history with romance. WAR CRY (Bantam 1983) by Donald Clayton Porter is part of the White Indian series.

The sexy Westerns came to dominate the paperback market in the 1980s. Typical is LONGARM AND THE LONE STAR BOUNTY by Tabor Evans (Jove 1984). It combines the hero and heroine of two other Jove series.

bi-monthly schedule.

Aside from borrowing marketing techniques from romantic publishers, the sexy Western publishers claim a strong female readershp for their racy series.

The marketing seems to have worked. Paperback Western series proliferated in the early 1980s and some 45 of the 375 series recorded in this text are continuing to issue from their publishers.

Ironically, it was only with the arrival of the sexy cowboys that the cowgirl appeared — Fancy Hatch and Lone Star and Molly Owen among them. Women have not been well treated in the formula Western series; existing largely as sex objects, they have become even more so in their own series, which are strictly adult.

Marriage is an institution rare in paperback series. Hopalong Cassidy was one of the few cowboys happily wedded — for a while. A family atmosphere marked the early Chip of the Flying U stories, but few others.

If anyone has been more poorly treated than women in these Westerns, it is native Americans. Until recently, Indians appeared mainly as villains. Indeed, the brutal character of Indian heroes such as Sundance and Apache show little has changed. White Squaw, a new series featuring a sex-starved Indian woman, offers the worst of both worlds.

Hispanic characters are found in Zorro and Don Ricardo in Ray Hogan's Rogue Bishop series. But except for Coco Bean in the Buchanan books, Whitton in the Rancho Bravo series and Strong in the Gringos series, there are almost no blacks.

Also interested in sex, in moderation, are the sprawling family sagas such as The Dakotas and Wagons West, which have claimed the romantic side of the Western field. Some are historically serious works, such as Vilhelm Moberg's The Emmigrants, translated from the Swedish, or Manfred's Buckskin Man tales.

Koontz speculated that "...More than any other category, the Western is condemned out of hand by people who make judgments without experience... Modern Western writers can and do turn out high-quality novels..."

Indeed the Western series needs no literary defense if it is achieving a primary goal: entertainment.

LIST OF WORKS CONSULTED

Adams, Les and Buck Rainey, *Shoot 'Em Ups* (Arlington House 1978)

Bleiler, E.F., introduction to *Eight Dime Novels* (Dover 1974)

Books in Print, various editions (R.R. Bowker)

Cawelti, John G., *The Six-Gun Mystique* (Bowling Green University Popular Press no date)

Children's Literature Research Collection, *Girls Series Books 1900-1975* (University of Minnesota Libraries 1978)

Contemporary Authors, various volumes (Gale Research)

Dary, David, *Cowboy Culture: A Saga of Five Centuries* (Avon 1981)

Davis, Kenneth C., *Two-Bit Culture: The Paperbacking of America* (Houghton-Mifflin 1984)

Dinan, John A., *The Pulp Western* (Borgo Press 1983)

Drew, Bernard A., "Sex in the Saddle," *Gallery,* December 1981

Drew, Bernard A., "A roundup of cowboys in PB book series published in the United States from 1933 to 1984," *Comics Buyer's Guide,* September 28, 1984.

Easton, Robert, *Max Brand The Big "Westerner"* (University of Oklahoma Press 1970)

Estleman, Loren D., "Westerns: Fiction's Last Frontier," *The Writer,* July 1981

Fiedler, Leslie A., *Love and Death in the American Novel* (Stein and Day 1975)

Gonzales, Arturo F., "Louis L'Amour: Writing High in the Bestseller Saddle," *Writer's Digest,* December 1980

Goulart, Ron, *An Informal History of the Pulp Magazines* (Ace 1973)

Gruber, Frank, *The Pulp Jungle* (Sherbourne Press 1967)

Gruber, Frank, *Zane Grey* (World Publishing 1970)

Hancer, Kevin, *The Paperback Price Guide* No. 2 (Harmony Books 1982)

Heide, Robert and John Gilman, *Cowboy Collectibles* (Harper & Row 1982)

Hudson, Henry K., *A Bibliography of Hard-Cover Series Type Boys' Books* (Data Print 1977)

Jonas, Larry, "The Return of the Dime Novel Heroes," *West Coast Review of Books,* January 1985.

Jones, Daryl, *The Dime Novel Western* (The Popular Press 1978)

Kanigher, Robert, *How to Make Money Writing for Magazines, Newspapers, Radio, Movies, Stage, Books, Comics* (Cambridge House 1943)

Knight, Damon, introduction to *Western Classics from the Great Pulps* (Bobbs-Merrill 1977)

Koontz, Dean R., *Writing Popular Fiction* (Writer's Digest 1972)

Lorton, Douglas, "Selling Western Stories," *Writer's Digest,* March 1932

Machalaba, Daniel, "The Old Gunslinger Becomes a Swinger in Adult Westerns," *Wall Street Journal,* July 15, 1981

Maule, Harry E., introduction to *Great Tales of the American West* (Modern Library 1945)

McNeil, Alex, *Total Television* (Penguin 1984)

Milton, John R., *The Novel of the American West* (University of Nebraska Press 1980)

Monaghan, Jay, *The Great Rascal: The Exploits of the Amazing Ned Buntline* (Bonanza Books 1961)

Murray, Will, "The Lone Ranger Rides the Pages of the Pulps," *Comics Buyers Guide*, May 11, 1984

Nevins, Allan, introduction to *James Fenimore Cooper's Leatherstocking Saga* (Modern Library 1966)

Nevins, Francis M. Jr., "Hopalong vs. Hoppy," *The Films of Yesteryear* No. 6, 1981

Nye, Russell, *The Unembarrassed Muse: The Popular Arts in America* (The Dial Press 1970)

Prager, Arthur, *Rascals at Large or, The Clue in the Old Nostalgia* (Doubleday 1971)

Rothel, David, *Who Was That Masked Man? The Story of the Lone Ranger* (A.S. Barnes 1976)

"Saddle up, Pardner. It's Gonna Take a Posse to Corral This Spring Roundup of Westerns," *Publisher's Weekly*, March 7, 1980

Sampson, Robert, *Yesterday's Faces vol. 1 Glory Figures* (Bowling Green University Popular Press 1983)

Sampson, Robert, *Yesterday's Faces vol. 2 Strange Days* (Bowling Green University Popular Press 1984)

Schreuders, Piet, *Paperbacks USA: A Graphic History 1939-1959* (Blue Dolphin Enterprises 1981)

Sonnichsen, C.L., *From Hopalong to Hud: Thoughts on Western Fiction* (Texas A&M University Press 1978)

Swanson, H.N. introduction to *Luke Short's Best of the West* (Arbor House 1983)

Tompkins, Walker A., "Preparing for a Career as a Western Pulp Writer," *Writer's Digest*, June 1938.

Tuska, Jon, *The American West in Fiction* (New American Library 1982)

Tuska, Jon, *The Filming of the West* (Doubleday 1976)

Tuska, Jon, "The Westerner Returns," *West Coast Review of Books*

Tuska, Jon and Vicki Piekarski, editors, *Encyclopedia of Frontier and Western Fiction* (McGraw-Hill 1983)

Vinson, James and D.K. Kirkpatrick, editors, *Twentieth-Century Western Writers* (Gale Research 1982)

Weinberg, Robert and Lohr McKinstry, *The Hero Pulp Index* (Opar Press 1971)

Williamson, Derek, "Shoot 'Em Up!" *The New York Times Book Review*, November 10, 1974

Ybarra, I.R., "The Western Heroes," *The Mystery & Adventure Series Review*, fall 1981

Zinman, David, *Saturday Afternoon at the Bijou* (Arlington House 1973)

ABOUT THIS BIBLIOGRAPHY

This bibliography of Western series and sequels was compiled with the first objective of identifying all such English-language entries and the second objective of listing such entries as accurately and completely as possible. Some series have no doubt been missed, and there are some gaps and perhaps a few errors. As information arrives, these details will be corrected in a future edition.

The compiler used a broad definition of Western in selecting entries for the book. For the bulk of the series, the hero lives in the late 19th century, wears a Stetson hat, Levi pants and a Colt revolver. Frontier novels, Canadian northland and Mountie novels, Mexican tales, French & Indian War and Civil War series and Western-setting romance sagas are included; colonial sagas, sea war and Revolutionary War adventures and Southern plantation novels generally are not. Juvenile as well as adult series are listed.

The 375 or so listings in the bibliography are based primarily on examination of books published in the United States, publisher catalogs and *Books in Print*. For some British series, it relies as well on earlier listings in *Twentieth Century Western Writers* and *Encyclopedia of Frontier and Western Fiction*. Information about boys' and girls' books was supplemented by information in *A Bibliography of Hard-Cover Series Type Boys' Books* and *Girls Series Books 1900-1975*.

The entries are arranged alphabetically by first major word in the series name or the last name of the leading character. The Spanish Bit Saga series will be found under S, for example, and Ranger Jim Hatfield under H.

The entries are arranged according to series, with all due apologies to the writers, because so many were published under pseudonyms. An appendix lists all authors and pseudonyms and their respective series for cross-reference. Book titles are also indexed. When known, dates and publishers are given for both United States and Great Britain or Canada or Australia first editions and mention is made of subsequent reprint editions. Where a pseudonymous author is known, the name is given in parenthesis in an entry. Where a title was changed in a subsequent edition, it is listed second in the entry.

1

LIST OF AUTHORS

BEARDSLEY, Charles
Making of America

BEECHER, Elizabeth
Roy Rogers

BELL, Robert
Rush McCowan

BENNETT, Billy L.
Northwest Stories

BENTEEN, John
Cutler
Fargo
Sundance

BICKHAM, Jack L.
Cam and Clayt
Wildcat O'Shea
Charity Ross
Slocum

BISHOP, Lee
American Explorers

BISHOP, Pike
Diamondback

BITTNER, Rosanne F.
Savage Destiny

BLACKBURN, Tom W.
Stanton Saga

BLANCHARD, Amy E.
Revolutionary Series

BLAUSEN, Peter J.
American Explorers

BONEHILL, Capt. Ralph
Frontier Series
Mexican Series

BORG, Jack
Hogleg Bailey

BOWER, B.M.
Chip of Flying U

BOYER, G.G.
Morgette

BRADEN, James
Braden Series
Indian Series

BRADY, William S.
Hawk I
Peacemaker

BRAND, Max
Dan Barry
Silvertip
Thunder Moon

BRAUN, Matt
Luke Starbuck

BRONTE, Louisa
American Dynasty

BROWN, Kitt
Frontier Women

BROWNE, George Waldo
Woodrangers

BURROUGHS, Edgar Rice
War Chief

CAIN, Jackson
Torn Slater

CALHOUN, Chad
Agent Brad Spear

CAMERON, Lou
Longarm
Making of America
Renegade
Doc Travis

CARSON, Capt. James
Saddle Boys

CARTER, Forrest
Josey Wales

CHADWICK, Joseph
Carmody

CHANDLER, Frank
Man With No Name

CHARBONNEAU, Lewis Henry
Blaine

CHASE, Josephine
Grace Harlowe

CHENEY, S. Lancer
Powder Valley

CHESTER, William L.
Kioga, the Snow Hawk

CHISHOLM, Matt
Blade
McAllister
Storm

CHRISTIAN, Frederick H.
Angel
Sudden

CLANCY, Eugene A.
Masked Rider

CLAY, John Wood
Hopalong Cassidy

CLAY, M. Jefferson
Brazos

CLEMENS, Samuel L.
Tom Sawyer

CLINTON, Jeff
Emerald Canyon
Wildcat O'Shea

CLUMPER, Mick
American Indians

COBURN, L.J.
Thorn

CODY, Al
Montana

CODY, Stetson
Cactus Clancy

COLE, Jackson
Jim Hatfield I
Jim Hatfield II
Rio Kid II

COLLINS, James L.
Colt Revolver

COLT, Clem
Pony George

CONNOR, Ralph
Corporal Cameron
Glengarry

CONROY, Al
Clayburn

COOK, Will
Cavalry Trilogy

COOPER, James Fenimore
Hawkeye

CORD, Barry
Town Tamer

COX, Stephen Angus
Dare Boys

COX, William R.
Bonanza
Buchanan

CRAFTON, Dennis
Lobo

CULP, John H.
Tail End

CUNNINGHAM, Chet
Chisholm
Agent Brad Spear
Jim Steel

CURRY, Gene
Jim Saddler

CURRY, Tom
Masked Rider
Rio Kid II

CURTIS, Alice Turner
Frontier Girl
Yankee

CURWOOD, James Oliver
Three Rivers

CUTTER, Tom
Tracker

DAILEY, Janet
Calder Saga

DANA, Mitchell
Dakota Bush

DANCER, J.B.
Lawman I

DAVIS, Don
Rio Kid I

DAVIS, Kathryn
Dakotas

DEAN, Les
Zorro

DeANDREA, William L.
Making of America

DENISON, Muriel
Susannah

DENVER, Lee
Dave Halloran
Cheyenne Jones

DICKS, Terrence
Mounties

DIXON, Dorothy
Leather and Lace

DOUGLAS, Thorne
Rancho Bravo

DRAGO, Harry Sinclair
Powder Valley

DRESSER, Davis
Twister Malone
Powder Valley
Rio Kid I

DUNN, Byron Archibald
Young Kentuckians
Young Missourians
Young Virginians

DUNNING, Hal
White Wolf

EAST, Fred
Powder Valley

ECKERT, Allan W.
Narratives of America

EDSON, J.T.
Brady Anchor
Calamity Jane
Civil War Stories
Floating Outfit
Cap Fog
Ole Devil Hardin
Rockabye County
John Slaughter
Waxahachie Smith
Waco

ELKINS, H.V.

Cutler

ELLIS, Wesley
Lone Star

EMERSON, Lucien M.
Powder Valley

ERSKINE, Laurie Y.
Renfrew

ESTLEMAN, Loren D.
Page Murdock

EVANS, Evan
Montana Kid

EVANS, Tabor
Longarm
Longarm and Lone Star

FANNIN, Cole
Roy Rogers

FAUST, Frederick
Dan Barry
Bill Hunter
Montana Kid
Silvertip
Thunder Moon

FERGUSSON, Harry
Santa Fe Trail

FERRIS, James Cody
X-Bar-X

FIELD, Peter
Powder Valley

FIELDHOUSE, W.L.
Gun Lust
Klaw
Six-Gun Samurai

FISHER, Clay
Tall Man

FISHER, Vardis

Vridar Hunter

FLETCHER, Aaron
Bounty Hunter
Making of America

FLETCHER, Dirk
Spur I

FLOREN, Lee
Lemuel Bates
Buckshot McGee

FLYNN, John
Gunsmoke

FORBES-LINDSEY, H.C.
Trail Blazers

FOREMAN, L.L.
Rogue Bishop

FORVE, Guy
American Explorers

FOSTER, Jeanne
Frontier Women

FOWLER, Frank
Broncho Rider Boys

FOX, Brian
Alias Smith and Jones
Man With No Name
Sabata

FOX, Genevieve May
Mountain Girl

FRANK, Lee
Kane

FRAZEE, Steve
Bonanza
High Chaparrel
Zorro

FRIEND, Ed
High Chaparrel

FRITCH, Elizabeth
California Saga

GARDINER, Dorothy
Sheriff Moss Magill

GARFIELD, Brian
Buchanan
Jeremy Six
Sam Watchman

GARLAND, John
Ross Grant

GENTRY, Buck
Scout

GILES, Janice Holt
Novels American Frontier

GILMAN, George G.
Adam Steele
Edge
Edge Meets Steele
Undertaker

GLIDDEN, Frederick D.
Big Jim Wade

GOLDSMITH, Don
Spanish Bit

GORDON, Charles William
Corporal Cameron
Glengarry

GOULART, Ron
Faro Blake
Agent Brad Spear

GRANGER, Georgia
Making of America

GREGOR, Elmer Russell
Eastern Indian
Jim Mason
Western Indian

GREENBERG, Martin H.
Best of the West
Reel West

GREENFIELD, Irving A.
Tom Carey

GREY, Loren
Buck Duanne
Lassiter I

GREY, Romer Zane
Arizona Ames
Buck Duanne
Nevada Jim Lacy
Laramie Nelson
Yaqui

GREY, Zane
Arizona Ames
At Stake-A Continent
Buck Duane
Nevada Jim Lacy
Adam Larey
Lassiter I
Laramie Nelson
Yaqui

GROVER, Marshall
Larry and Stretch
Nevada Jim

GRUBER, Frank
Tales of Wells Fargo

GUNN, Tom
Sheriff Blue Steele

GUTHRIE, A.B.
Western Quintet

HAAS, Ben L.
Cutler
Fargo
Rancho Bravo
Sundance

HAMILTON, Bob
  Gene Autry

HANSEN, Peter
  American Indian

HARDIN, J.D.
  Raider and Doc

HARDIN, John W.
  Fargo

HARKNETT, Terry
  Apache
  Jubal Cade
  Edge
  Edge Meets Steele
  Man With No Name

HARMON, Fred
  Red Ryder

HARRIS, Larry
  Masked Rider

HARRISON, C. William
  Masked Rider
  Rio Kid II

HART, William S.
  Boys' Golden West

HARVEY, John B.
  Apache
  Hart
  Herne
  Lawman I
  Peacemaker
  Steele
  Thorn
  Undertaker

HAWK, Alex
  Elfego O'Reilly

HAWKES, Zachery
  Fancy Hatch

HAWKINS, Edward H.

Al Palmer

HAYES, Lee
  Agent Brad Spear

HAYES, Ralph
  Buffalo Hunter

HENDRYX, James B.
  Corporal Downey
  Halfaday Creek
  Connie Morgan

HENRY, Will
  Great Indian Warriors

HERSCHMAN, Morris
  Kilburn

HEUMAN, William
  Mulvane

HILL, Morgan
  Dan Colt

HILLERMAN, Tony
  Sgt. Jim Chee
  Lt. Joe Leaphorn

HOBART, Donald Baynes
  Masked Rider

HOBSON, Francis Thayer
  Powder Valley

HOGAN, Ray
  Doomsday Marshal
  Shawn Starbuck

HOGAN, Robert J.
  Powder Valley

HOLLIDAY, Joe
  Dale of Mounted

HONIG, Donald
  Jed McLane

HORGAN, Paul
Mountain Standard

HOTCHKISS, Bill
American Indians

HOWARD, John Wesley
Easy Company

HOWARD, Robert E.
Breckinridge Elkins

HUNT, Greg
American Explorers
Making of America
Ridge Parkman

HUNTER, E.J.
White Squaw

HUTCHINSON, W.H.
Gene Autry

INGALLS, Laura Wilder
Little House

INGRAHAM, Col. Prentiss
Buffalo Bill

JAKES, John
Bicentennial

JAMES, Cy
Spur II

JAMES, Lawrence
Apache

JAMES, Leigh Franklin
Saga of Southwest

JAMES, William M.
Apache

JEIER, Thomas
Matt Bishop

JESSUP, Richard
Wyoming Jones

JOSCELYN, Archie C.
Montana

KELLEY, Leo P.
Cimarron
Making of America
Luke Sutton

KELTON, Elmer
Tales of Texas

KETCHUN, Philip
Cabot

KIRK, Matthew
Claw

KITTREDGE, William
Cord

KNOTT, Will C.
Longarm
Vengeance Seeker

KOZLOW, Mark J.
Devlin

KRASSNER, William
American Explorers

KRAUZER, Steven M.
Blaze
Cord

L'AMOUR, Louis
Bowdrie
Hopalong Cassidy
Sacketts

LANGE, Dietrich
Indian Stories

LANGLEY, John
Walt Warren

LAROM, Henry V.
Mountain Pony

LAWRENCE, Fred
American Explorers

LAWRENCE, Steven C.
Slattery

LAYMAN, Richard
Making of America

LeBEAU, Roy
Buckskin

LEDD, Paul
Shelter

LEDERER, Paul Joseph
Indian Heritage

LEE, Howard
Kung Fu

LEE, Patrick
Six-Gun Samurai

LEE, Steve
Sloane

LEE, Tammy
Leather and Lace

LEWIS, Alfred Henry
Wolfeville

LOGAN, Jake
Slocum

LONGTREE, Warren T.
Ruff Justice

LOOMIS, Noel
Bonanza
Have Gun, Will Travel
Tales of Wells Fargo

LORD, Tom
Ash Tallman

LOUNSBERRY, Lt. Lionel

Rob Ranger

LUND, Trygve
Dick Weston

LYNDE, Stan
Latigo

MacDONALD, William Colt
Gregory Quist
Three Mesquiteers

MacDOWELL, Syl
Sherriff Blue Steele

MAJORS, E.B.
Slaughter and Son

MANFRED, Frederick
Buckskin Man

MANN, E.B.
Powder Valley
Whistler

MANNING, David
Ronicky Doone
Bill Hunter

MARSHALL, Mel
Longarm

MARTIN, Cort
Bolt

MASTERS, Zeke
Faro Blake

MASTERSON, Louis
Morgan Kane

MAY, Karl
Old Shatterhand

McCARTHY, Gary
Derby Man
Lone Ranger
Wind River

McCOY, Marshall
  Larry and Stretch
  Nevada Jim

McCULLEY, Johnston
  Zorro

McCURTIN, Peter
  Carmody
  Rainey
  S u n d a n c e

McGILL, Jerry
  Red Ryder

McELROY, Lee
  Tales of Texas

McINTYRE, John T.
  Buckskin Books

McLAGLEN, John J.
  Herne

McMAHAN, Ian
  Making of America

MEARS, Leonard F.
  Larry and Stretch
  Nevada Jim

MEYER, Karl H.
  American Indians

MIDDLETON, Don
  Roy Rogers

MILLARD, Joe
  Man With No Name
  Hec Ramsey

MILLER, Albert G.
  Fury

MILLER, Basil
  Ken
  Patty Lou

MILLER, Jim
  Colt Revolver

MILLER, Snowden
  Gene Autry
  Roy Rogers

MILLS, Robert E.
  Kansan

MINES, Samuel
  Powder Valley

MITCHUM, Hank
  Stagecoach Station

MOBERG, Vilhelm
  Emigrants

MOORE, Amos
  Quicksilver

MOORE, Arthur
  Alamo

MOORE, Paula
  Making of America

MORGAN, G.J.
  Dunne
  Lomax
  Railroads

MULFORD, Clarence E.
  Hopalong Cassidy
  Corson of JC

MURRAY, Ken
  Ben Dawson

MYER, Karl
  Making of America

MYERS, Barry
  Making of America

NEWMAN, Paul S.

Gunsmoke

NEWSOM, Ed
Brannigan I

NEWTON, D.B.
Bannister
Eden Grove
Logan

NEWTON, Mike
Bounty Man
Lawman II

NICKERSON, Arthur T.
Reuben Brown
Rusty Hines

NOLAN, Frederick
Angel

NORMAN, David
Frontier Rakers

NUSBAUM, Deric
Deric

NYE, Nelson
Pony George
Wild Horse Shorty

O'BANYON, Constance
Savage Romance

O'BRIAN, Jack
Silver Chief

OBSTFELD, Raymond
Diamondback

OKE, Janette
Prairie Romance

OLD SCOUT
Young Wild West

O'REILLY, Jackson
American Indians

OWEN, Dean
Latigo
Hec Ramsey
Rio Kid II
Virginian

OVERHOLSER, Stephen
Molly Owens

PALMER, Bernard
Breck

PARKER, F.M.
Coldiron

PARKER, Laurie
American Explorers

PATCHIN, Frank Gee
Pony Rider
Range and Grange

PATTEN, Gilbert
Don Kirk

PATTEN, Lewis B.
Gene Autry

PAYNE, Oliver
Northwest Territory

PEHRSON, Howard
Slocum

PIKE, Charles R.
Jubal Cade

POOLE, Helen Lee
Whitewater Dynasty

PORTER, Donald Clayton
American Indians
White Indian

POWERS, Paul S.
White Wolf

PROCTOR, George W.

Texians

PRONZINI, Bill
Best of the West
Reel West

QUIN, Dan
Wolfeville

RANDALL, Clay
Amos Flagg

RANDISI, Robert J.
Gunsmith
Tracker

RANDOLPH, Forrest A.
Confederate

RATHBONE, St. George
Ranch and Range

RAYMOND, James
American Explorers

REESE, John
Hewitt

RENO, Clint
Vigilante

REPP, Ed Earl
Powder Valley

RICHARDS, Milton
Dick Kent

RICHARDS, Tad
Making of America

RICHMOND, Roe
Lashtrow

RISTEEN, H.L.
Indian Stories for Boys

RIVERS, Jim
Roy Rogers

ROBERTS, J.R.
Gunsmith

ROBERTS, Mark K.
Six-Gun Samurai

ROBERTSON, Frank G.
Have Gun, Will Travel

RODERUS, Frank
Harrison Wikle

ROLVAAG, O.E.
Immigrant Trilogy

ROOSEVELT, Capt. Wyn
Frontier Boys

ROSENSTOCK, Janet
Story of Canada

ROSS, Dana Fuller
Wagons West

ROTHWEILER, Paul R.
Westward Rails

ROUNTREE, Owen
Cord

ROWE, J.G.
Northwest Stories

ROWLAND, Donald S.
Lomax
Dunne

RUBEL, James L.
Medico

RUSSELL, Charles M.
Rawhide Rawlins

RYAN, Tom
Brannigan II

SABIN, Edward L.
Bar B

Trail Blazers

SANDERS, Brett
Hawk II

SANDON, J.D.
Gringos

SCOTT, A. Leslie
Jim Hatfield I
Walt Slade

SCHISGALL, Oscar
Jim Hatfield II

SCOTT, Bradford
Walt Slade

SEAFIELD, James
Making of America

SHAPPIRO, Herbert A.
Canavan
Mustang Marshal

SHARPE, Jon
Trailsman

SHEARS, Judith
American Indians

SHERMAN, Jory
Bolt
Gunn

SHERRIFFS, Gordon D.
Gunsmoke
Lee Kershaw
Quint Kershaw

SHERWOOD, Elmer
Buffalo Bill II

SHORT, Luke
Jim Wade

SIEGEL, Scott
Warhunter

SILVERBERG, Robert
Buchanan

SLADE, Jack
Lassiter II
Sundance

SMITH, Carl W.
Red Ryder

SMITH, George
American Freedom

SMITH, Martin Cruz
Slocum

SMITH, Russell
Yuma

SNELL, Leroy
Northwest Stories

SNOW, Charles H.
Rim-Fire
Thorne

SOMMERS, Jeanne
American Indians
Making of America

SOTONA, Wayne
High Chaparrel

STEELE, Gunnison
Rio Kid II

STERRETT, Frances R.
Tales

STEVENS, S.S.
Red Ryder

STRANGE, Oliver
Sudden

STRATEMEYER, Edward
Colonial Series I

STRATTON, Chris
Gunsmoke

STRIEB, Daniel
Women of the West

STRIKER, Fran
Gene Autry
Lone Ranger
Roy Rogers

TAYLOR, Janelle
Indian Ecstasy

TELFAIR, Richard
Wyoming Jones

THOMAS, H.C.
Red Ryder

THOMPSON, Thomas
Bonanza

THORNE, Ramsey
Renegade

TIPPETTE, Giles
Wilson Young

TOMLINSON, Everett T.
American Scouting
Colonial Series II
Great American Indian Chiefs
Pioneer Scout
War for Union

TOMLINSON, Paul G.
Great American Indian Chiefs

TOMPKINS, Walker A.
Masked Rider
Paintin' Pistoleer
Rio Kid II
Roy Rogers
White Wolf

TOOMBS, John
American Indians

Making of America

TRIMNELL, Robert L.
Loner

TURNER, Clay
Ben Gold

TURNER, Robert
Gunsmoke

TURNER, Robert Harry
Ben Dawson

TUTTLE, W.C.
Conroy
Hashknife Hartley
Sad Sontag

TWAIN, Mark
Tom Sawyer

TYLER, Zack
Foxx

VANDERCOOK, Margaret
Ranch Girls

VAUGHAN, Robert
Making of America

VICTOR, Sam
Kilburn

WAGER, Walter
Making of America

WALDO, Dave
Johnny Ross

WALES, Mike
Leatherhand

WALL, Robert E.
Canadians

WALLMAN, Jeffrey
Matt Bishop

Bronc

WARD, Jonas
Buchanan

WARREN, George A.
Musket Boys

WATTS, Peter Christopher
Blade
McAllister
Storm

WAYNE, Les
Arvada Jones

WEBB, Jean Francis
Making of America

WEBER, Catherine
American Indians

WELLS, Lee E.
Rio Kid II

WESTON, Matt
Drifter Morgan

WHITE, Stewart Edward
Saga of Andy Burnett
Orde Family
Saga of California

WHITED, Charles
Spirit of America

WHITMAN, S.E.
Captain Apache

WHITTINGTON, Harry
Longarm

WILKINS, Dale
Long Trail

WILLIAMS, Edward Huntington
Red Plume

WILLIAMS, Jeanne
Arizona Saga

WILLOUGHBY, Lee Davis
Making of America
Women of the West

WILSON, Harry Leon
Red Gap

WINSTAN, Matt
Reuben Brown

WINTERBOTHAM, R.R.
Red Ryder

WINTERS, Logan
Spectros

WINTHER, Sophus K.
Grimsen

WISTER, Owen
Virginian

WOODLEY, Richard
American Explorers

WYATT, Zach
Texians

WYCHOFF, James
John Slaughter

WYNNE, Brian
Jeremy Six

YOUNG, Carter Travis
Blaine

YOUNG, Egerton Ryerson
Three Boys

YOUNG, Gordon
Red Clark

ZACHERY, Elizabeth
Making of America

WESTERN SERIES AND SEQUELS

1. ALAMO
By Arthur Moore
Alamo is a gunslinger.
A Man Called Alamo (Pinnacle 1975)
Night Riders (Pinnacle 1978)

2. ALIAS SMITH AND JONES
By Brian Fox
The series was based on the 1971-73 television series about two outlaws,
Hannibal Hayes/Joshua Smith and Kid Curry/Thaddeus Jones, trying to
earn amnesty by assuming new identities and keeping out of trouble.
Fox was a penname for W.T. Ballard.
The Outlaw Trail (Award 1969)
Unholy Angel (Award 1969)
Dead Ringer (Award 1971)
Apache Gold (Award 1971)
Dragooned (Award 1971)

3. AMERICAN DYNASTY SERIES
By Louisa Bronte
This saga series features a different family in each book.
The Vallette Heritage (Jove)
The Van Rhyne Heritage (Jove)
The Gunther Heritage (Jove 1981)

4. AMERICAN EXPLORERS
Various Authors
The series features the exploits of frontiersmen. It was published under
the Emerald imprint.
1. Jed Smith, Freedom River by Fred Lawrence (Dell 1981)
2. Lewis & Clark, Northwest Glory by James Raymond (Dell 1981)
3. Jim Bridger, Mountain Man (Dell)
4. Daniel Boone, Westward Trail by Neal Barrett Jr. (Dell)
5. John Fremont, California Bound by Michael Beahan (Dell)
6. Kit Carson, Trapper King by Laurie Parker (Dell)
7. Zebulon Pike, Pioneer Destiny by Richard Woodley (Dell)
8. Marcus Whitman, Frontier Misson by Greg Hunt (Dell 1982)
9. Francis Parkman, Dakota Legend by William Krassner (Dell 1982)
10. Escalante, Wilderness Path by Peter T. Blausen (Dell)
11. Davy Crockett, Frontier Fighter by Lee Bishop (Dell 1983)
12. Alexander Mackenzie, Lone Courage by Guy Forve (Dell 1983)
13. John Bozeman, Mountain Journey by Hunt (Dell 1983)
14. Joseph Walker, Frontier Sheriff by Lawrence (Dell 1983)

5. AMERICAN FREEDOM
By George Smith
This saga is about the Glencannons — patriots, sinners, lovers and fighters.
The Devil's Breed (Playboy)
The Rogues (Playboy)
The Fire Brands (Playboy 1980)

6. AMERICAN INDIANS
Various Authors
The series spotlights different tribes in each volume. Published under the Standish imprint.
1. Comanche Revenge by Jeanne Sommers (Dell 1981)
2. Blackfoot Ambush by Catherine Weber (Dell 1981)
3. Crow Warriors by Bill Hotchkiss (Dell 1981)
4. Chippewa Daughter by Jane Toombs (Dell 1982)
5. Creek Rifles by Peter Hansen (Dell 1982)
6. Cheyenne Raiders by Jackson O'Reilly (Dell 1982)
7. Cherokee Mission by Karl H. Meyer (Dell 1982)
8. Apache War Cry by Donald Porter (Dell 1982)
9. Sioux Arrows by Porter (Dell 1982)
10. Nez Perce Legend by Mick Clumper (Dell 1983)
11. Kowa Fires by Porter (Dell 1983)
12. Shoshone Thunder by Hotchkiss and Judith Shears (Dell 1983)
13. Arapaho Spirit by Toombs (Dell 1983)
14. Pawnee Medicine by Hotchkiss and Shears (Dell 1983)

7. AMERICAN SCOUTING SERIES
By Everett T. Tomlinson
This is a boys' book series.
Pursuit of the Apache Chief (D. Appleton 1920)
Scouting on the Border (D. Appleton 1920)
The Mysterious Rifleman (D. Appleton 1921)
Scouting with Mad Anthony (D. Appleton 1922)
Scouting on the Old Frontier (D. Appleton 1923)
Scouting in the Wilderness (D. Appleton 1924)
Pioneer Scouts of the Ohio (D. Appleton 1924)
Scouting on Lake Champlain (D. Appleton 1925)
Scouting on the Mohawk (D. Appleton 1925)
Washington's Young Scouts (D. Appelton 1926)
Scouting in the Desert (D. Appelton 1927)
The Spy of Saragota (D. Appleton 1928)
Scouting with Daniel Boone (D. Appleton 1931)
Scouting with Kit Carson (D. Appleton 1931)

AMERICAN TRAIL BLAZERS
See TRAIL BLAZERS

8. ARIZONA AMES
By Zane Grey and Romer Zane Grey
Zane Grey's Rich Ames, hero of the 1930 novel *Arizona Ames,* was revived for a series of novelettes in *Zane Grey's Western Magazine.* The new stories were printed under the house name Romer Zane Grey (the real name of Grey's son). The books initially came out under the Tower imprint in 1980, then were re-issued by Leisure in 1984. The original Grey novel was issued in paperback by Pocket in 1973.
Arizona Ames by Zane Grey (Harper 1932)
Zane Grey's Arizona Ames: Gun Trouble on the Tonto Basin by Romer Zane Grey (Tower 1980)
Zane Grey's Arizona Ames: King of the Outlaw Horde by Romer Zane Grey (Tower 1980)

9. BRADY ANCHOR AND JEFFERSON TRADE
By J.T. Edson
This book was announced as being part of a series.
Two Miles to the Border (Corgi 1972)

10. FRANK ANGEL, FEDERAL MARSHAL
By Frederick H. Christian
The series about "the toughest lawman in the West" is said to be based on a real special investigator for the Department of Justice, Frank Warner Angel. The books were written by Frederick Nolan and were first published by Sphere Books in England, 1972-75. Zebra reprinted the series in the United States 1975-76, using the British titles. The books switched to the Pinnacle imprint, first using the same titles, then new ones. Zebra highlighted the name Angel on its cover design. Pinnacle's first version highlighted the title. Then it began a new version highlighting Frank Angel Federal Marshal (sub-titled "How the West Really Was") and re-titling the books, 1979-80. Then it switched to calling it the Justice Series, still using the new titles.
Find Angel (Sphere 1972) (Zebra 1974) Ride Clear of Daranga (Pinnacle 1979)
Kill Angel (Sphere 1972) (Zebra 1974) Bad Day at Agua Caliente (Pinnacle 1979)
Find Angel (Sphere 1973) (Zebra 1974) Ride Out to Vengeance (Pinnacle 1979)
Trap Angel (Sphere 1973) (Zebra 1974) Ambush in Purgatory (Pinnacle 1979)
Hang Angel (Sphere 1975) (Pinnacle 1975) Showdown at Trinidad (Pinnacle 1979)
Frame Angel (Sphere 1975) (Pinnacle 1975) Shoot-Out at Silver King (Pinnacle 1980)
Hunt Angel (Sphere 1975) (Pinnacle 1975) Massacre in Madison (Pinnacle 1980)
Take Angel (Sphere 1975) Warn Angel (Pinnacle 1975)
Stop Angel (Sphere 1976) (Pinnacle 1976)

11. APACHE
By William M. James
Apache, Cuchillo Oro (The Golden Knife), is an Indian warrior whose exploits are violent and bloody. The stories were written by Terry Harknett, Laurence James and John B. Harvey under the pseudonym. The books were also printed in England.
1. The First Death (by Terry Harknett) (Pinnacle 1974) (Sphere 1975)
2. Knife in the Night (by Harknett) (Pinnacle 1974) (Sphere 1975)
3. Duel to the Death (Pinnacle 1975) (Sphere 1975)
4. The Death Train (Pinnacle 1975)
5. Fort Treachery (by Harknett) (Pinnacle 1975) (Paramount 1975)
6. Sonora Slaughter (by Harknett) (Pinnacle 1976) (New English Library 1979)
7. Blood Line (Pinnacle 1976) (New English Library 1979)
8. Blood on the Tracks (by Harknett) (Pinnacle (1976) (New English Library 1979)
9. The Naked and the Savage (Pinnacle 1977) (New English Library)
10. All Blood is Red (by Harknett) (Pinnacle 1977) (New English Library 1980)
11. Cruel Trail (Pinnacle 1978)
12. Fool's Gold (Pinnacle 1978)
13. Best Man (by Harknett) (Pinnacle 1979)
14. Born to Die (Pinnacle 1979)
15. Blood Rising (by John B. Harvey) (Pinnacle 1979)
16. Texas Killing (Pinnacle 1980)
17. Blood Brother (by Harvey) (Pinnacle 1980)
18. Slow Dying (Pinnacle 1980)
19. Fast Living (Pinnacle 1981)
20. Death Dragon (by Harvey) (Pinnacle 1981)
21. Blood Wedding (Pinnacle 1981)
22. Border Killing (Pinnacle 1982)
23. Death Valley (Pinnacle 1983)
24. Death Ride (Pinnacle 1983)
25. Times Past (Pinnacle 1983)
26. The Hanging (Pinnacle 1983)
27. Debt of Blood (Pinnacle 1984)

12. ARIZONA SAGA
By Jeanne Williams
Women are featured in this saga series.
The Valiant Women (Pocket 1980)
Harvest of Fury (Pocket 1981)
Mating of Hawks (Pocket 1982)

13. AT STAKE — A CONTINENT
By Zane Grey
The author's first three historical novels, published in hardcover in 1903

(Charles Francis Press), '06 (Burt) and '09 (Burt), based on the story of his ancestors the Zanes, were packaged as a series by this juvenile publisher. The titles are also found in other paperback editions from other publishers.
1. Betty Zane (Tempo, no date)
2. The Spirit of the Border (Tempo, no date)
3. The Last Trail (Tempo, no date)

14. GENE AUTRY
Various Authors
The popular B-Western movie star was featured in a series of juvenile hardcover books.
Gene Autry and the Thief River Outlaws by Bob Hamilton (Fran Striker) (Whitman 1946)
Gene Autry and the Redwood Pirates by Hamilton (Striker) (Whitman, 1946)
Gene Autry and the Golden Ladder Gang by W.H. Hutchinson (Whitman 1950)
Gene Autry and the Badmen of Broken Bow by Snowden Miller (Whitman 1951)
Gene Autry and the Big Valley Grab by Hutchinson (Whitman 1952)
Gene Autry and the Ghost Riders by Lewis B. Patten (Whitman 1955)
Gene Autry and the Golden Stallion by Patten (Whitman 1957)

15. HOGLEG BAILEY
By Jack Borg
Charles Proudfoot "Hogleg" Bailey is a range detective in this British series.
Gunsmoke Feud (Jenkins 1957)
Kansas Trail (Jenkins 1958)
Badlands Fury (Jenkins 1959)
Rustlers' Range (Jenkins 1959)
Range Wolves (Jenkins 1960)
Saddle Tramp (Jenkins 1960)
Horsethieves Hang High (Jenkins 1961)
Kid with a Colt (Jenkins 1961)
Guns of the Lawless (Jenkins 1962)
Cast a Wide Loop (Jenkins 1963)
Texas Wolves (Jenkins 1963)
Gun Feud at Sun Creek (Jenkins 1964)
Rope for a Rustler (Jenkins 1965)

16. JIM BANNISTER
By D.B. Newton
Bannister has a $12,000 price tag on his head. Dwight Bennett Newton wrote the series. Some entries were also published in large-type editions.

On the Dodge (Berkley 1962)
The Savage Hills (Berkley 1964)
Bullets in the Wind (Berkley 1964)
The Manhunters (Berkley 1966)
Hideout Valley (Berkley 1967)
The Wolf Pack (Berkley 1968)
The Judas Horse (Berkley 1969)
The Syndicate Gun (Berkley 1972)
Range Tramp (Berkley 1973)
Bounty on Bannister (Berkley 1975)
Broken Spur (Berkley 1977)

17. BAR B SERIES
By Edward L. Sabin
This is a boys' book series.
The Bar B Boys or, The Young Cowpunchers (Crowell 1909)
Range and Trail or, The Bar B's Great Drive (Crowell 1910)
Circle K or, Fighting for the Flock (Crowell 1911)
Old Four-Toes or, The Hunters of the Peaks (Crowell 1912)
Treasure Mountain or, The Young Prospectors (Crowell 1913)
Scarface Ranch or, The Young Homesteaders (Crowell 1914)

18. WHISTLIN' DAN BARRY
By Max Brand
Frederick Faust wrote this series under his most famous pseudonym.
The first appeared in the pulp *Argosy All-Story Weekly* beginning
December 7, 1919. *The Seventh Man* also appeared in *Argosy* as a six-
part serial. Pocket re-issued the books in paperback.
The Untamed (Putnam 1919)
The Night Horseman (Putnam 1920)
The Seventh Man (Putnam 1921)
Dan Barry's Daughter (Putnam 1924)

19. JUDGE LEMUEL BATES
By Lee Floren
Judge Lemuel Bates is a young, tough defender of the law in the
teritories. Tobacco Jones is his sidekick. The series has had at least three
publishers.
Wyoming Showdown (Lancer 1970)
Bonanza at Wishbone (Belmont Tower 1971)
Guns of Montana (Leisure 1980)
Puma Pistoleers (Leisure 1980)
Double Cross Ranch (Leisure 1981)

20. BEST OF THE WEST
Edited by Bill Pronzini and Martin H. Greenberg
Each collection of short stories has a theme.
The Lawmen (Fawcett 1984)

The Outlaws (Fawcett 1984)
The Cowboys (Fawcett 1985)
The Warriors (Fawcett 1985)
The Railroaders (Fawcett 1986)
The Steamboaters (Fawcett 1986)

21. BICENTENNIAL SERIES
By John Jakes
Some of the entries in this bestselling saga series are set in the West.
The Bastard (Pyramid 1974) (Corgi 1975, 2 volumes)
The Rebels (Pyramid 1975) (Corgi 1979)
The Seekers (Pyramid 1975) (Corgi 1979)
The Furies (Pyramid 1976) (Corgi 1979)
The Titans (Pyramid 1976) Corgi 1979)
The Warriors (Pyramid 1977) (Corgi 1979)
The Lawless (Jove 1978) Corgi 1979)
The Americans (Jove 1980) (Corgi?)

22. MATT BISHOP
By Thomas Jeier and Jeffrey Wallman
The books are about a young man on the run in California following a
bank robbery.
Return to Conta Lupe (Doubleday 1983)
The Celluloid Kid (Doubleday 1984)

23. ROGUE BISHOP
By L.L. Foreman
Rogate "Rogue" Bishop, gunman, cardsharp and adventurer, is fre-
quently joined by the self-styled aristocrat Don Ricardo. The stories
were reprinted in Ace and Ace Charter editions.
Spanish Grant (Doubleday 1962)
The Mustang Trail (Doubleday 1965)
The Silver Flame (Doubleday 1966)

24. BLADE
By Matt Chisholm
The books were written pseudonymously by Peter Christopher Watts.
The Indian Incident (Hamlyn 1978)
The Tucson Conspiracy (Hamlyn 1978)
The Pecos Manhunt (Hamlyn 1979)
The Laredo Assignment (Hamlyn 1979)
The Colorado Virgins (Hamlyn 1979)
The Mexican Proposition (Hamlyn 1979)
The Nevada Mustang (Hamlyn 1979)
The Arizona Climax (Hamlyn 1980)
The Cheyenne Trap (Hamlyn 1980)
The Montana Deadlock (Hamlyn 1980)
The Navaho Trail (Hamlyn 1981)

The Last Act (Hamlyn 1981)

25. BLAINE
By Carter Travis Young
Cullom Blaine is the full name of the cowboy hero, and Louis Henry
Charbonneau is the real name of the author. The hardcover series has
been reprinted by Belmont Tower and Dell.
Blaine's Law (Doubleday 1974)
Red Grass (Doubleday 1976)
Winter Drift (Doubleday 1980)

26. FARO BLAKE
By Zeke Masters
This series features a professional gambler. The author is a pseudonym
for Ron Goulart and others. In a departure, the adult series in one entry,
Call the Turn, spotlighted an ongoing woman character, doxy Nell
Gavin.
1. The Big Gamble (Pocket 1980)
2. The Luck of the Draw (Pocket 1980)
3. Threes Are Wild (Pocket 1980)
4. Diamond Flush (Pocket 1981)
5. Riverboat Showdown (Pocket 1981)
6. Four of a Kind (Pocket 1981)
7. Bottom Deal (Pocket 1981)
8. Ace in the Hole (Pocket 1981)
9. Boomtown Bustout (Pocket 1981)
10. Mexican Standoff (Pocket 1981)
11. Six-Gun Poker (Pocket 1981)
12. Devil's Jackpot (Pocket 1982)
13. Fast Shuffle (Pocket 1982)
14. Full House (Pocket 1982)
15. Place Your Bets (Pocket 1982)
16. Stacked Deck (Pocket 1982)
17. Sucker Bet (Pocket 1982)
18. High Card (Pocket 1982)
19. Call the Turn (Pocket 1982)
20. Inside Straight (Pocket 1982)
21. Deuces to Open (Pocket 1982)
22. Loaded Dice (Pocket 1982)
23. Long Odds (Pocket 1982)
24. Stagg Night (Pocket 1982)
25. Close to the Vest (Pocket 1983)
26. Texas Two-Step (Pocket 1983)
27. Down and Dirty (Pocket 1983)
28. Cashing In (Pocket 1983)
29. Double or Nothing (Pocket 1983)
30. Devil's Gambit (Pocket 1983)
31. Up for Grabs (Pocket 1983)

27. BLAZE
By J.W. Baron
The first of what was announced as an adult series, by Steven M. Krauzer, was never continued.
  Blaze (Pinnacle 1983)

28. BLUE PETE
By Luke Allan
William Lacey Amy, an Englishman living in Canada, wrote this series. The hero is an ex-cattle rustler who works undercover for the Royal Canadian Mounted Police.
  Blue Pete, Half Breed: A Story of the Cowboy West (Jenkins 1920)
  The Return of Blue Pete (Jenkins 1922) (McCann 1921)
  Blue Pete, Detective (Jenkins 1928) (Doran 1922)
  Blue Pete, Horsethief (Jenkins 1938)
  The Vengeance of Blue Pete (Jenkins 1939)
  Blue Pete, Rebel (Jenkins 1940)
  Blue Pete Pays a Debt (Jenkins 1942)
  Blue Pete Breaks the Rules (Jenkins 1943)
  Blue Pete, Outlaw (Jenkins 1944)
  Blue Pete's Dilemma (Jenkins 1945)
  Blue Pete to the Rescue (Jenkins 1947)
  Blue Pete's Vendetta (Jenkins 1947)
  Blue Pete and the Pinto (Jenkins 1948)
  Blue Pete Works Alone (Jenkins 1948)
  Blue Pete, Unofficially (Jenkins 1949)
  Blue Pete, Indian Scout (Jenkins 1950)
  Blue Pete at Bay (Jenkins 1952)
  Blue Pete and the Kid (Jenkins 1953)
  Blue Pete Rides the Foothills (Jenkins 1953)
  Blue Pete in the Badlands (Jenkins 1954)

29. BOLT
By Cort Martin
Jared Bolt is a gunman and outlaw in this adult series by Jory Sherman.
  1. First Blood (Zebra 1981)
  2. Dead Man's Bounty (Zebra 1981)
  3. Showdown at Black Mesa (Zebra 1981)
  4. The Guns of Taos (Zebra 1981)
  5. Shootout at Santa Fe (Zebra 1982)
  6. Tombstone Honeypot (Zebra 1982)
  7. Rawhide Woman (Zebra 1982)
  8. Hard in the Saddle (Zebra 1982)
  9. Badman's Bordello (Zebra 1983)
  10. Bawdy House Showdown (Zebra 1983)
  11. The Last Bordello (Zebra 1983)
  12. The Hangtown Harlots (Zebra 1983)
  13. Montana Mistress (Zebra 1984)

14. Virginia City Virgin (Zebra 1984)
15. Bordello Backshooter (Zebra 1984)
16. Hardcase Hussy (Zebra 1985)
17. Lone-Star Stud (Zebra 1985)
18. Queen of Hearts (Zebra 1985)

30. BONANZA
Various Authors
The Bonanza books were based on the long-running (1959-73) television series about the Cartwright family — patriarch Ben and sons Adam, Hoss and Little Joe — and their huge Ponderosa Ranch.
   Bonanza by Noel Loomis (Popular 1960)
   Bonanza 1: One Man With Courage by Thomas Thompson (Media Books 1966)
   Bonanza 2: Black Gold by William R. Cox (Media Books 1966)
   Killer Lion by Steve Frazee (Whitman 1966)
   Treachery Trail (Whitman 1968)

BORDER PEACE OFFICER
   See JABE LOMAX

31. BOUNTY HUNTER
By Aaron Fletcher
Jake Coulter seeks revenge for the deaths of his parents.
   1. Bounty Hunter (Leisure 1977)
   2. Blood Money (Leisure 1977)

32. BOUNTY MAN
By Mike Newton
Matt Price was a town marshal until raiders savaged it, and his wife. He now hunts outlaws for the money.
   1. Bounty Man (Carousel Westerns)
   2. Massacre Trail (Carousel Westerns 1979)

33. BOWDRIE
By Louis L'Amour
The Chick Bowdrie, Texas Ranger stories were originally published in *Popular Western* in the 1940s. The author has provided new, historical background material as introductions to many of the stories.
   Bowdrie (Bantam 1983)
   Bowdrie's Law (Bantam 1984)

34. BOY RANCHERS
By Willard F. Baker
This is a boys' book series.
   The Boy Ranchers or, Solving the Mystery at Diamond X (Cupples and Leon 1921)
   The Boy Ranchers in Camp or, The Water Fight at Diamond X (Cup-

ples and Leon 1921)
   The Boy Ranchers on the Trail or, The Diamond X After Cattle
Rustlers (Cupples and Leon 1921)
   The Boy Ranchers Among the Indians or, Trailing the Yaquis (Cupples
and Leon 1922)
   The Boy Ranchers at Spur Creek or, Fighting the Sheep Herders (Cup-
ples and Leon 1923)
   The Boy Ranchers in the Desert or, Diamond X and the Lost Mine
(Cupples and Leon 1924)
   The Boy Ranchers on Roaring River or, Diamond X and the Chinese
Smugglers (Cupples and Leon 1926)
   The Boy Ranchers in Death Valley or, Diamond X and the Poison
Mystery (Cupples and Leon 1928)
   The Boy Ranchers in Terror Canyon or, Diamond X Winning Out
(Cupples and Leon 1930)

BOYS OF THE ROYAL MOUNTED POLICE
   See DICK KENT SERIES

35. BOYS' GOLDEN WEST SERIES
   By William S. Hart
This is a boys' book series.
   Injun and Whitey (Houghton Mifflin 1920)
   Injun and Whitey Strike Out for Themselves (Houghton Mifflin 1921)
   Injun and Whitey to the Rescue (Houghton Mifflin 1922)

36.BRADEN SERIES
   By James Braden
This is a boys' book series.
   Far Past the Frontier (Saalfield 1902)
   Connecticut Boys in the Western Reserve (Saalfield 1903)
   Captives Three (Saalfield 1904)
   The Trail of the Seneca (Saalfield 1907)

37. BRANNIGAN (I)
   By Ed Newsom
Chagro Brannigan is a Texas rancher.
   1. Brannigan (Zebra 1981)
   2. Comanchero Chase (Zebra 1981)
   3. Blood Bullets (Zebra 1982)
   4. The Peacekeeper (Zebra 1983)

38. BRANNIGAN (II)
   By Tom Ryan
"No jail could hold him, no woman's bed could trap him," proclaims a
cover blurb.
   1. Brannigan (Leisure 1974)
   2. The Man from Furnace Creek (Leisure 1975)

3. Mark of the Rattler (Leisure 1975)

39. BRAZOS
    By M. Jefferson Clay
During the Civil War, Hank Brazos fought for the Confederacy, Duke Benedict for the Union. Now the two are united fighting outlaws.
    Adios, Bandido/Desperados on the Loose (Belmont Tower double 1976)
    Aces Wild/Badge for Brazos (Tower double 1980)

40. BRECK
    By Bernard Palmer
The series is issued by a Christian publishing house. John Breckinridge, a deadly gunman, has changed his name to John Breck and is seeking a new life on a ranch, without his gun. But then his livelihood and family are threatened. The series was published in the United States by Living Books beginning in 1984, in Canada by Horizon Westerns beginning in 1981. An examination of the first title from both publishers finds the book was totally rewritten for the U.S. market.
    Breck's Choice (Horizon House 1981) (Living Books 1984)
    Hunted Gun (Living Books 1984)
    Kid Breckinridge (Living Books 1984)

41. BRONC
    By Jeffrey M. Wallman
Bronc is a bounty hunter in this adult entry announced as the first in a series.
    1. Brand of the Damned (Leisure 1982)

42. BRONCHO RIDER BOYS
    By Frank Fowler
This is a boys' book series.
    The Broncho Rider Boys at Keystone Ranch or, Three Chums of the Saddle and Lariat (A.L. Burt 1914)
    The Broncho Rider Boys Down in Arizona or, A Struggle For the Great Copper Lode (A.L. Burt 1914)
    The Broncho Rider Boys Along the Border or, The Hidden Treasure of the Zuni Medicine Man (A.L. Burt 1914)
    The Broncho Rider Boys on the Wyoming Trail or, The Mystery of the Prairie Stampede (A.L. Burt 1914)
    The Broncho Rider Boys with the Texas Rangers or, The Smugglers of the Rio Grande (A.L. Burt 1915)
    The Broncho Rider Boys with Funston at Vera Cruz or, Upholding the Honor of the Stars and Stripes (A.L. Burt 1916)

43. REUBEN BROWN
    By Matt Winstan
The English series features the rancher Brown and Henderson City. The

books were written pseudonymously by Arthur T. Nickson.
Bandit Trail (Jenkins 1962)
Trail to Boot Hill (Jenkins 1962)
No Branding Fire (Jenkins 1963)
Guns at Salt Flats (Jenkins 1964)

44. BUCHANAN
By Jonas Ward
Four writers have taken turns as Jonas Ward in this long-running series.
William R. Cox introduced companion Coco Bean, a champion black
boxer. Tom Buchanan is a big, amiable drifter. The character was
featured in a motion picture, "Buchanan Rides Alone" (1958), starring
Randolph Scott.
The Name's Buchanan (by William Ard) (Fawcett 1956)
Buchanan Says No (by Ard) (Fawcett 1957)
Buchanan Gets Mad (by Ard) (Fawcett 1958)
One-Man Massacre (by Ard) (Fawcett 1958)
Buchanan's Revenge (by Ard) (Fawcett 1960)
Buchanan on the Prod (by Ard and Robert Silverburg) (Fawcett (1960)
Buchanan's Gun (by Brian Garfield) (Fawcett 1968)
Buchanan's War (by William R. Cox) (Fawcett 1971)
Trap for Buchanan (by Cox) (Fawcett 1972)
Buchanan's Gamble (by Cox) (Fawcett 1973)
Buchanan's Siege (by Cox) (Fawcett 1973)
Buchanan on the Run (by Cox) (Fawcett 1974)
Get Buchanan (by Cox) (Fawcett 1974)
Buchanan Takes Over (by Cox) (Fawcett 1975)
Buchanan Calls the Shots (by Cox) (Fawcett 1975)
Buchanan's Big Showdown (by Cox) (Fawcett 1976)
Buchanan's Texas Treasure (by Cox) (Fawcett 1977)
Buchanan's Stolen Railway (by Cox) (Fawcett 1978)
Buchanan's Manhunt (by Cox) (Fawcett 1979)
Buchanan's Range War (by Cox) (Fawcett 1980)
Buchanan's Big Fight (by Cox) (Fawcett 1981)
Buchanan's Black Sheep (by Cox (Fawcett 1985)

45. BUCKSKIN
By Roy LeBeau
Buckskin Frank Leslie is a deadly gun on the run in this adult series.
1. Rifle River (Leisure 1984)
2. Gunstock (Leisure 1984)
3. Pistoltown (Leisure 1984)
4. Colt Creek (Leisure 1984)
5. Gunsight Gap (Leisure 1985)
6. Trigger Spring (Leisure 1985)
7. Cartridge Coast (Leisure 1985)
8. Hangfire Hill (Leisure 1985)
9. Crossfire Country (Leisure 1985)

10. Bolt-Action (Leisure 1986)

46. BUCKSKIN BOOKS
By John Thomas McIntyre
This is a boys' book series.
In the Rockies with Kit Carson (Penn 1913)
In Kentucky with Daniel Boone (Penn 1913)
In Texas with Davy Crockett (Penn 1914)
On the Border with Andrew Jackson (Penn 1915)

47. BUCKSKIN MAN TALES
By Frederick Manfred
This series of frontier stories contains many historical details. It was
reprinted in paperback by Signet.
Lord Grizzley (McGraw Hill 1954)
Riders of Judgment (Random House 1957)
Conquering Horse (McDowell Obolensky 1959)
Scarlet Plume (Simon and Shuster 1964)
King of Spades (Simon and Shuster 1966)

48. BUFFALO BILL (I)
By the Author of Buffalo Bill
Plainsman and scout Buffalo Bill (Col. William Frederick) Cody was first
featured in dime novel tales in 1869, when he was only 23. His exploits
were recounted in *Buffalo Bill Stories, Buffalo Bill Border Stories* and
New Buffalo Bill Weekly. In the 1960s (the books are undated), Gold
Star reprinted stories from *Buffalo Bill Stories.* Along with a Buffalo Bill
story from the Street & Smith magazine, each volume also featured a
James Boys story from *Wide Awake Library.* The books announced
more than 30 in the series. Listed are ones confirmed to have been
printed. A Buffalo Bill story from a different dime novel was included in
Eight Dime Novels edited by E.F. Bleiler (Dover 1974): "Adventures of
Buffalo Bill from Boyhood to Manhood" by Colonel Prentiss Ingraham
(Beadle's *Boy's Library of Sport, Story and Adventure* Vol. 1 No. 1
December 14, 1881).
Buffalo Bill's Spy Shadower (Gold Star)
Buffalo Bill's Leap for Life (Gold Star)
Buffalo Bill's Raid of Death (Gold Star)
Buffalo Bill's Feather Weight (Gold Star)
Buffalo Bill's Tomahawk Duel (Gold Star)
Buffalo Bill's Trouble (Gold Star)
Buffalo Bill's Fair, Square Deal (Gold Star)

49. BUFFALO BILL (II)
By Elmer Sherwood
This is a boys' book series penned by Samuel Lewenkrohn.
Buffalo Bill's Childhood (Whitman 1919)

Buffalo Bill and the Pony Express (Whitman 1919)

50. BUFFALO HUNTER
By Ralph Hayes
O'Brien, the Buffalo Hunter, is a loner. The first in the series appeared in hardcover. The books were issued, with some variations in title, by Belmont Tower and Manor.
The Name is O'Brien (Lenox Hill, 1972) O'Brien — Buffalo Hunter: Hellhole (Belmont Tower 1973)
O'Brien — Buffalo Hunter: Four Ugly Guns (Belmont Tower 1973) Vengeance is Mine (Manor 1978)
O'Brien — Buffalo Hunter: Gunslammer (Belmont Tower 1973) The Secret of Sulphur Creek (Manor)

51. SAGA OF ANDY BURNETT
By Stewart Edward White
The frontier series was collected in a single volume (last entry).
The Long Rifle (Doubleday 1932) (Hodder & Stoughton 1932)
Ranchero (Doubleday 1933) (Hodder & Stoughton 1933)
Folded Hills (Doubleday 1934) (Hodder & Stoughton 1934)
Stampede (Doubleday 1942) (Hale 1952)
The Saga of Andy Burnett (Doubleday 1947)

52. DAKOTA BUSH
By Mitchell Dana
Young Dakota Bush is learning from Garrett, the rugged gunfighter who has taken him under his wing. Myron Danow wrote the series.
Beyond the Law (Avon 1972)
Town Without a Prayer (Avon 1972)
The Last Buffalo (Avon 1973)
Gun Shy (Avon 1973)
Incident in a Texas Town (Avon 1975)
Beware the Smiling Stranger (Avon 1977)

53. CABOT
By Philip Ketchum
Cabot is a hard-nosed cowboy.
1. The Man Who Tamed Dodge (Lancer 1967)
2. The Man Who Turned Outlaw (Lancer 1967)
3. The Man Who Sold Leadville (Lancer 1968)
Cabot (Lancer 1969)

54. JUBAL CADE
By Charles R. Pike
Cade is a doctor seeking revenge. The violent series was written by Terry Harknett and others and published originally in England. The first 13 titles were reprinted in the United States by Chelsea House in 1980.
1. The Killing Trail (by Terry Harkett) (Mayflower 1974) (Chelsea

House 1980)
2. Double Cross (by Harknett) (Mayflower 1974) (Chelsea House 1980)
3. The Hungry Gun (by Harknett) (Mayflower 1975) (Chelsea House 1980)
4. Killer Silver (Chelsea House 1980)
5. Vengeance Hunt (Chelsea House 1980)
6. The Burning Man (Chelsea House 1980)
7. The Golden Dead (Chelsea House 1980)
8. Death Wears Grey (Chelsea House 1980)
9. Days of Blood (Chelsea House 1980)
10. The Killing Ground (Chelsea House 1980)
11. Brand of Vengeance (Chelsea House 1980)
12. Bounty Road (Chelsea House 1980)
13. Ashes and Blood (Granada 1979) (Chelsea House 1980)
14. The Death Pit (Granada)
15. Angel of Death (Granada)
16. Mourning is Red (Granada)
17. Bloody Christmas (Granada)
18. The Time of the Damned (Granada)
19. The Waiting Game (Granada)
20. Spoils of War (Granada)
21. The Violent Land (Granada 1983)

55. CALAMITY JANE
By J.T. Edson
The stories of Martha Jane Canary, or Calamity Jane, were published in England. Bantam tested the waters in the U.S. with one volume. See also *The Wildcats* in the Floating Outfit series.
Trouble Trail (Brown Watson 1965)
The Cow Thieves (Brown Watson 1965)
The Bull Whip Breed (Brown Watson 1965) (Bantam 1969)
The Big Hunt (Brown Watson 1967)
Calamity Spells Trouble (Corgi 1968)
Cold Deck, Hot Lead (Corgi 1969)
White Stallion, Red Mare (Corgi 1970)
The Remittance Kid (Corgi 1978)
The Whip and the War Lance (Corgi 1979)
Calamity, Mark and Belle (Corgi announced)
Cut One, They All Bleed (Corgi announced)
J.T.'s Ladies (Corgi 1980)

56. CALDER SAGA
By Janet Dailey
This series, issued initially in hardcover by the same publisher, is available in paperback in two cover versions, one showing a passionate scene from the old West, the other a collage suggesting more modern times.
This Calder Sky (Pocket 1982)
This Calder Range (Pocket 1982)
Stands a Calder Man (Pocket 1983)
Calder Born, Calder Bred (Pocket 1984)

57. CALIFORNIA SAGA
By Elizabeth Fritch
This is a Western romance saga series.
Passion's Trail (Zebra)
Golden Fires (Zebra)
A Heart Divided (Zebra)

58. CALLAHAN
By Francis H. Ames
Tom Conroy (hardcover) or Conway (soft) is the hero of this Callahan series. Ace reprinted the first title in paperback.
That Callahan Spunk (Doubleday 1965)
Callahan Goes South (Doubleday 1976)
The Callahans Gamble (Doubleday)

59. CAM AND CLAYT
By Jack M. Bickham
John Campbell and Clayton Hartung are trail pards.
Gunman's Gamble (Ace 1958)
Feud Fury (Ace 1959)
Killer's Paradise (Ace 1959)
The Useless Gun (Ace 1960)
Gunmen Can't Hide (Ace 1961)
Hangman's Territory (Ace 1961)

60. CORPORAL CAMERON
By Ralph Connor
Charles William Gordon wrote these Mountie books under a penname.
Corporal Cameron: A Tale of the North-West Mounted Police (Westminster 1912) (Hodder & Stoughton 1912)
The Patrol of the Sun Dance Trail (Doran 1914) (Hodder & Stoughton 1914)

61. THE CANADIANS
By Robert E. Wall
This saga is about the Nowell family in an untamed land.
1. Blackrobe (Bantam)
2. Bloodbrothers (Bantam)
3. Birthright (Bantam)
4. Patriots (Bantam 1982)
5. Inheritors (Bantam 1983)
6. Dominion (Bantam 1984)
7. The Acadians (Bantam 1984)

8. The Brotherhood (Bantam 1985)

62. CANAVAN
By Burt Arthur and Budd Arthur
Johnny "Red" Canavan is an ex-Texas Ranger. The books were first written singly by Burt Arthur (Herbert Arthur Shappiro), then jointly with Budd Arthur. *The Texan* was first published in hardcover, then reprinted in paperback. There have been four paperback publishers.
The Texan by Burt Arthur (Robert M. McBride & Co. 1946)
Walk Tall, Ride Tall by Burt Arthur (Signet 1963)
Gunsmoke in Nevada by Burt Arthur (Avon 1963)
Return of the Texan (Magnum)
Canavan's Trail by Burt and Budd Arthur (Leisure 1980)
Action at Truxton by Burt and Budd Arthur (Avon 1965)

63. CAPTAIN APACHE
By S.E. Whitman
Captain Cullah Burnett of the U.S. Cavalry is a fearless Indian fighter.
Captain Apache (Berkley)
Change of Command (Berkley 1966)

64. TOM CAREY
By Irving A. Greenfield
Tom Carey is seeking revenge.
The Carey Blood (Dell 1972)
Carey's Vengeance (Dell 1972)
The Carey Gun (Dell 1974)

65. CARMODY
By Joseph Chadwick and Peter McCurtin
Carmody is an outlaw featured in a series which has been issued by Belmont Tower, Leisure and Unibooks. The first book listed below may not be related to the series, though it shares the character's name and is from the same publisher; this book is in the first person, the McCurtin series is in the third person. According to *Twentieth Century Western Writers*, McCurtin rewrote the Carmody books and sold them as a new series, Jim Saddler as by Gene Curry.
Carmody by Joseph Chadwick (Tower 1969)
1. The Slavers by Peter McCurtin (Belmont Tower 1971)
2. The Killers by McCurtin (Belmont Tower)
3. Tough Bullet by McCurtin (Belmont Tower)
4. Tall Man Riding by McCurtin (Belmont Tower)
5. Hang Town by McCurtin (Belmont Tower)
6. Screaming on the Wire by McCurtin (Belmont Tower 1972)

66. HOPALONG CASSIDY
By Clarence E. Mulford and Tex Burns
Anyone familiar with the Hopalong Cassidy film series (66 pictures from

1935-48) and television program (1951-52) starring William Boyd wouldn't recognize the character to read Mulford's original, realistic Western novels. In the books, Cassidy cusses, spits tobacco juice and is less than a role model for youngsters.

The series began as stories in *Outing Magazine*, collected in book form in 1907 and followed by 17 novels. The books, featuring an assortment of running characters such as Mesquite Jenkins, Buck Peters, Red Connors, Johnny Nelson and Tex Ewalt, were issued in inexpensive hardcover editions and in softcover by 10 publishers.

There were also four boys' books in the series, issued at the height of the television program's popularity, by Tex Burns (Louis L'Amour), and a pulp magazine, *Hopalong Cassidy's Western*, also appeared, carrying the Burns tales. All but four of Mulford's Cassidy books were reprinted in paper; not re-issued were *Bar-20, The Coming of Cassidy, Johnny Nelson* and *Mesquite Jenkins.* Aeonian Press reprinted the Mulford books in hardcover.

Bar-20 (Outing 1907) (Hodder and Stoughton 1922) Hopalong Cassidy's Rustler Round-Up (Grosset & Dunlap 1950)

Hopalong Cassidy (Hodder and Stoughton 1920) (McCLurg 1910) Bar-20 Days (McClurg 1911) (Hodder and Stoughton 1921) Hopalong Cassidy's Private War (Grosset & Dunlap 1950)

Buck Peters, Ranchman with John Wood Clay (McClurg 1912) (Hodder and Stoughton 1921)

The Coming of Cassidy — And the Others (McClurg 1913) (Hodder and Stoughton 1921) The Coming of Hopalong Cassidy (Grosset & Dunlap 1950)

The Man from Bar-20: A Story of the Cow-Country (McClurg 1918) (Hodder and Stoughton 1921)

Johnny Nelson (McClurg 1920) (Hodder and Stoughton 1921)

The Bar-20 Three (McClurg 1921) (Hodder and Stoughton 1921) Hopalong Cassidy Sees Red (Grosset & Dunlap 1950)

Tex (McClurg 1922) Tex — of Bar-20 (Hodder and Stoughton 1922) Hopalong Cassidy Returns (Doubleday 1924) (Hodder and Stoughton 1924)

Hopalong Cassidy's Protege (Doubleday 1926) (Hodder and Stoughton 1926) Hopalong Cassidy's Saddlemate (Popular 1949)

The Bar-20 Rides Again (Doubleday 1926) (Hodder and Stoughton 1926) Hopalong Cassidy's Bar-20 Rides Again (Doubleday 1950)

Mesquite Jenkins (Doubleday 1928) (Hodder and Stoughton 1928)

Hopalong Cassidy and the Eagle's Brood (Doubleday 1931) (Hodder and Stoughton 1931)

Mesquite Jenkins, Tumbleweed (Doubleday 1932) (Hodder and Stoughton 1932)

Trail Dust (Doubleday 1934) (Hodder and Stoughton 1934) Hopalong Cassidy with the Trail Herd (Doubleday 1950)

Hopalong Cassidy Takes Cards (Doubleday 1937) (Hodder and Stoughton 1938)

Hopalong Cassidy Serves a Writ (Doubleday 1941) (Hodder and

Stoughton 1942)
    Hopalong Cassidy and the Riders of High Rock by Tex Burns (Doubleday 1951) (Hodder and Stoughton 1952)
    Hopalong Cassidy and the Rustlers of West Fork by Burns (Doubleday 1951) (Hodder and Stoughton 1951)
    Hopalong Cassidy's Trail to Seven Pines by Burns (Doubleday 1951) (Hodder and Stoughton 1952)
    Hopalong Cassidy, Trouble Shooter by Burns (Doubleday 1952) (Hodder and Stoughton 1953)

67. CAVALRY TRILOGY
By Will Cook
This trilogy is about the United States Cavalry and the Indians.
    Commanche Captives (Bantam 1960)
    The Peacemakers (Bantam 1961)
    The Outcasts (Bantam 1965)

68. SGT. JIM CHEE
By Tony Hillerman
The hero is a contemporary Indian police officer. The books were issued in paper by Avon.
    People of Darkness (Harper 1980) (Gollancz 1982)
    The Dark Wind (Harper 1982) (Gollancz 1983)
    Ghostway (Harper 1984)

69. CHIP OF THE FLYING U
By B.M. Bower
Bertha M. Bower wrote a realistic series of hardcover novels about ranch life, beginning in 1906. Series stories first ran in *Popular Magazine* and *Argosy*. Several were reprinted in paperback. Featured were Chip Bennett and his pards, including Della Whitmore, a doctor. A 1949 motion picture, "Chip of the Flying U," featured Johnny Mack Brown.
    Chip of the Flying U (Dillingham 1906) (Nelson 1920)
    The Happy Family (Dillingham 1910) (Nelson 1920)
    The Flying U Ranch (Dillingham 1914) (Nelson 1921)
    The Flying U's Last Stand (Little, Brown 1915) (Hodder and Stoughton 1922)
    Dark Horse: A Story of the Flying U (Little, Brown 1931) (Hodder and Stoughton 1932)
    The Flying U Strikes (Little, Brown 1934) (Hodder and Stoughton 1934)

70. CHISHOLM
By Chet Cunningham
Raised by the Chiracahua, Wade Chisholm finds himself caught between the white and Indian cultures.
    1. Apache Ambush (Carousel Western, 1980)

2.
3. Man in Two Camps (Carousel Western 1980)

71. CIMARRON
By Leo P. Kelley and Lew Baines
A wanted man on the run, Cimarron is an adult series.
1. Cimarron and the Hanging Judge by Leo P. Kelley (Signet 1983)
2. Cimarron Rides the Outlaw Trail by Kelley (Signet 1983)
3. Cimarron and the Border Bandits by Kelley (Signet 1983)
4. Cimarron in the Cherokee Strip by Kelley (Signet 1983)
5. Cimarron and the Elk Soldiers by Kelley (Signet 1983)
6. Cimarron and the Bounty Hunters by Kelley (Signet 1983)
7. Cimarron and the High Riders by Kelley (Signet 1984)
8. Cimarron in the No Man's Land by Kelley (Signet 1984)
9. Cimarron and the Vigilantes by Kelley (Signet 1984)
10. Cimarron and the Medicine Wolves by Kelley (Signet 1984)
11. Cimarron on Hell's Highway by Kelley (Signet 1984)
12. Cimarron and the War Women by Kelley (Signet 1985)
13. Cimarron and the Bootleggers by Kelley (Signet 1985)
14. Cimarron on the High Plains by Lew Baines (Signet 1985)
15. Cimarron and the Prophet's People by Kelley (Signet 1985)
16. Cimarron and the Scalphunters by Kelley (Signet 1985)
17. Cimarron and the Comancheros by Baines (Signet 1985)
18. Cimarron and th Gun Hawk's Gold by Kelley (Signet 1985)
19. Cimarron on a Texas Manhunt by Baines (Signet 1986)
20. Cimarron and the Red Earth People by Kelley (Signet 1986)

72. CIVIL WAR SERIES
By Joseph A. Altsheler
This is a boys' book series.
The Guns of Bull Run (D. Appleton 1914)
The Guns of Shiloh (D. Appleton 1914)
The Scouts of Stonewall (D. Appleton 1914)
The Sword of Antietam (D. Appleton 1914)
The Star of Gettysburg (D. Appleton 1915)
The Rock of Chicamaugua (D. Appleton 1915)
The Shades of the Wilderness (D. Appleton 1916)
The Tree of Appomattox (D. Appleton 1916)

73. CIVIL WAR STORIES
By J.T. Edson
First Lieutenant Dusty Fog of the Texas Light Cavalry (later to join the writer's Floating Outfit series) was the hero of this British paperback series.
The Fastest Gun in Texas (Brown Watson 1963)
The Devil Gun (Brown Watson 1966) (Bantam 1969)
The Colt and the Sabre (Brown Watson 1967)

Comanche (Brown Watson 1967) (Berkley 1978)
The Rebel Spy (Corgi 1968)
The Bloody Border (Corgi 1969) (Berkley 1978)
Under the Stars and Bars (Corgi 1970)
Kill Dusty Fog! (Corgi 1970)
Back to the Bloody Border (Corgi 1970)
You're in Command Now, Mr. Fog (Corgi 1973)
The Big Gun (Corgi 1973)
A Matter of Honour (Corgi 1981)

74. JIM "CACTUS" CLANCY
By Stetson Cody
The main character has been a range detective and marshal.
Cactus Clancy Rides (W.H. Allen 1949)
Cactus Justice (W.H. Allen 1952)
Lawdog's Bite (W.H. Allen 1965)
The Gunslick Code (W.H. Allen 1965)
Guns Along the Ruthless (Hale 1973)

75. RED CLARK
By Gordon Young
Red Clark and his saddle pards Billy Haynes and Tom Jones were
featured in a hardcover series reprinted by Popular.
Red Clark O'Tulluco (Doubleday 1933) Roaring Guns (Popular Library
1949)
Red Clark Rides Alone (Doubleday 1933) Fast on the Draw (Popular
Library 1950)
Red Clark of the Arrowhead (Doubleday 1935) Guns of the Arrowhead
(Popular Library 1950)
Red Clark on the Border (Doubleday 1937) Trouble on the Border
(Popular Library 1951)
Red Clark, Range Boss (Doubleday 1938) Red Clark, Boss! (Methuen
1938) Range Boss (Popular Library 1951)
Red Clark, Two-Gun Man (Doubleday 1939) Two-Gun Man (Popular
Library 1952)
Red Clark for Luck (Doubleday 1940)
Red Clark Takes a Hand (Doubleday 1941)
Red Clark at the Showdown (Doubleday 1947)
Red Clark in Paradise (Doubleday 1947) Holster Law (Popular Library)
Gunman from Tulluco (Popular Library 1948)
Red Clark to the Rescue (Doubleday 1948) Hot Lead Trail (Thrilling
Books)
Fighting Blood (Popular Library 1949)

76. CLAW
By Matthew Kirk
This British paperback series features a gunman, Tyler Wyatt, who is
seeking revenge on the men who crippled him.

1. Day of Fury (Granada)
2. Vengeance Road (Granada)
3. The Wild Hunt (Granada 1983)

77. CLAYBURN
By Al Conroy
"Clay" Clayburn is a gambler and gunfighter. Marvin H. Albert is the author. Dell issued the series in two editions.
Clayburn (Dell 1961)
Last Train to Bannock (Dell 1963)
Three Rode North (Dell 1964)
The Man in Black (Dell 1965)

JIM CLEVE
See YAQUI

78. COLDIRON
By F.M. Parker
Mountain man and rancher Luke Coldiron's adventures were reissued by Signet in paperback.
Coldiron (Doubleday 1984)
Shadow of the Wolf (Doubleday 1985)

79. COLONIAL SERIES (I)
By Edward Stratemeyer
This is a boys' book series about the French and Indian War.
With Washington in the West or, A Soldier Boy's Battles in the Wilderness (Lee and Shepard 1901)
Marching on Niagara or, The Soldier Boys of the Old Frontier (Lee and Shepard 1902)
At the Fall of Montreal or, A Soldier Boy's Final Victory (Lee and Shepard 1903)
On the Trail of Pontiac or, Pioneer Boys of the Ohio (Lee and Shepard 1904)
The Fort in the Wilderness or, The Soldier Boys of the Indian Trails (Lee and Shepard 1905)
Trail and Trading Post or, The Young Hunters of the Ohio (Lee and Shepard 1906)

80. COLONIAL SERIES (II)
By Everett T. Tomlinson
These books are set during the French and Indian War.
With Flintlock and Fife (W.A. Wilde 1903)
The Fort in the Forest (W.A. Wilde 1904)
A Soldier of the Wilderness (W.A. Wilde 19059
The Young Rangers (W.A. Wilde 1906)

COLONIZATION OF AMERICA
See WHITE INDIAN

81. DAN COLT WESTERN SAGA
By Morgan Hill
Dan Colt is a cowboy on the run.
1. Twin Colts (Dell 1980)
2. The Quick and the Deadly (Dell 1980)
3. Boot Hill Brother (Dell 1981)
4. Ten Must Die (Dell 1981)
5. Bandits in Blue (Dell 1981)
6. The Midnight Hangman (Dell 1982)
? The Last Bullet (Dell 1982)
? Dead Man's Noose (Dell 1982)
? Last Stage to Eternity (Dell 1983)

82. COLT REVOLVER NOVELS
By Jim Miller
The novels feature the Callahan brothers and the Colts they carry as
they tame the Western frontier. The books are by James L. Collins.
Gone to Texas (Fawcett 1984)
Comanche Trail (Fawcett 1984)
War Clouds (Fawcett 1984)
Riding Shotgun (Fawcett 1985)
Orphans Preferred (Fawcett 1985)
Sunsets (Fawcett 1985)
Campaigning (Fawcett 1985)

83. THE CONFEDERATE
By Forrest A. Randolph
Griff Stark, a former Confederate soldier, searches the West for his son
Jeremy, who may be held by Indians in this adult series.
1. The Confederate (Zebra 1984)
2. Ride Beyond Glory (Zebra 1984)
3. Sabre Charge (Zebra 1985)
4. Blood Cavalry (Zebra 1985)

84. SHERIFF HENRY CONROY
By W.C. Tuttle
Henry Conroy is a former vaudevillian elected sheriff in Tonto County.
Entries in the series appeared in hardcover, paperback and pulp ver-
sions.
Wild Horse Valley (Houghton Mifflin 1938)
Henry the Sheriff (Houghton Mifflin 1936)
Galloping Gold (Collins 1961)

85. CORD
By Owen Rountree

Cord and Chi are a team like Bonnie and Clyde, bank robbers on the run. The series is copyright by William Kittredge and Steven M. Krauzer.

Cord (Ballantine 1982)
The Nevada War (Ballantine 1982)
The Black Hills Duel (Ballantine 1983)
King of Colorado (Ballantine 1984)
Gunman Winter (Ballantine 1984)
Hunt the Man Down (Ballantine 1984)
Gunsmoke River (Ballantine 1985)
Paradise Valley (Ballantine 1986)

86. CORSON OF THE JC
By Clarence E. Mulford
Bob Corson of the JC Ranch and his pals Nueces and Shorty are featured in this series, of which three books were reprinted in paper. Not reprinted was *On the Trail of the Tumbling T,* which spotlighted Nueces. Corson also appeared in *Hopalong Cassidy and the Eagle's Brood.*

Corson of the JC (Doubleday 1927)
Me 'n Shorty (Doubleday 1929)
The Deputy Sheriff (Doubleday 1930)
On the Trail of the Tumbling T (Doubleday 1935)

JOSHUA CREED
See LAWMAN

87. CUTLER
By Various Authors
John Cutler is a mountain man and hunter. His adventures were issued in Belmont Tower and Tower editions.
1. Wolf Pack by John Benteen (Ben Haas) (Belmont Tower 1972)
2. The Gunhawks by Benteen (Haas) (Belmont Tower 1974)
3.
4. Yellowstone (Tower)
5.
6. Tiger's Chance by H.V. Elkins (Tower 1980)

88. THE DAKOTAS
By Kathryn Davis
The series is about building an empire in the Dakota Badlands.
1. The Dakotas: At the Wind's Edge (Pinnacle 1983)
2. The Dakotas: The Endless Sky (Pinnacle 1984)

89. DALE OF THE MOUNTED
By Joe Holliday
This series of hardcover juvenile books, issued in Canada, features Royal Canadian Mounted Police Constable Dale Thompson.
Dale of the Mounted (Thomas Allen)
Dale of the Mounted in the Arctic (Thomas Allen 1953)

Dale of the Mounted on the West Coast (Thomas Allen 1954)
Dale of the Mounted in Newfoundland (Thomas Allen 1955)
Dale of the Mounted in the Northwest (Thomas Allen 1958)
Dale of the Mounted — Atlantic Assignment (Thomas Allen 1959)
Dale of the Mounted — Atomic Plot (Thomas Allen 1959)
Dale of the Mounted — Dew Line Duty (Thomas Allen)
Dale of the Mounted — Submarine Hunt (Thomas Allen)
Dale of the Mounted — In Hong Kong (Thomas Allen 1962)
Dale of the Mounted on the St. Lawrence (Thomas Allen)
Dale of the Mounted at the U.N. (Thomas Allen)

90. DARE BOYS
By Stephen Angus Cox
This is a Revolutionary War boys' book series with some entries set on
the frontier.
The Dare Boys of 1776 (A.L. Chatterton 1910)
The Dare Boys on the Hudson (A.L. Chatterton 1910)
The Dare Boys in Trenton (A.L. Chatterton 1910)
The Dare Boys on the Brandywine (A.L. Chatterton 1910)
The Dare Boys in the Red City (A.L. Chatterton 1910)
The Dare Boys After Benedict Arnold (A.L. Chatterton 1910)
The Dare Boys in Virginia (A.L. Chatterton 1910)
The Dare Boys with General Greene (A.L. Chatterton 1910)
The Dare Boys with Lafayette (A.L. Chatterton 1910)
The Dare Boys with the Swamp Fox (A.L. Chatterton 1910)
The Dare Boys at Vincennes (A.L. Chatterton 1911)
The Dare Boys in the North West (A.L. Chatterton 1912)

91. MARSHAL BEN DAWSON
By Ken Murray
Robert Harry Turner penned these books under a pseudonym. The
lawman of Piney Flats was featured in a television program called "The
Marshal's Daughter" featuring actor Ken Murray.
Hellion's Hole/Feud in Piney Flats (Ace Double 1953)

92. DEERSLAYER
By James Fenimore Cooper
The Leatherstocking Tales featuring the frontier (at that time New York
State) adventures of Deerslayer, real name Natty Bumppo, also known
as Hawkeye and Pathfinder, and his Indian companion Chingachgook.
The books have been frequently reprinted.
The Pioneers (1823)
The Last of the Mohicans (1826)
The Prairie (1827)
The Pathfinder (1840)
The Deerslayer (1841)

DENVER DAN
See YOUNG WILD WEST

93. THE DERBY MAN
By Gary McCarthy
Darby Buckingham is a dime novel writer from New York who becomes involved in Western adventures. Early escapades were first issued in hardcover and reprinted in paper by Dell.
The Derby Man (Doubleday 1976) (Hale 1978)
Showdown at Snakegrass Junction (Doubleday 1978) (Hale 1979)
Mustang Fever (Doubleday 1980)
The Pony Express War (Bantam 1980)
Silver Shot (Bantam 1981)
Explosion at Donner Pass (Bantam 1981)
Rebel of Bodie (Bantam 1982)
North Chase (Bantam 1982)
The Rail Warriors (Bantam 1983)

94. DERIC SERIES
By Deric Nusbaum
This is a boys' book series.
Deric in Mesa Verde (G.P. Putnam's 1926)
Deric with the Indians (G.P. Putnam's 1927)

95. DEVLIN
By Mark J. Kozlow
Chris Devlin is a gunfighter who has hung up his six-shooter.
Gunfighter's Trail (Carousel Westerns 1980)
The Hangtown Mistake (Carousel Westerns 1981)
The Gunfighter and the Tong Boss (Carousel Westerns 1981)
Devlin in the Canyon Heat (Carousel Westerns 1981)

96. DIAMONDBACK
By Pike Bishop
The series, copyright by Raymond Obstfeld, is about a cowboy whose real name is seen only on wanted posters. As Cord Diamondback, he's "blazed new fame as a judge-for-hire." This is an adult series.
1. Diamondback (Pinnacle 1983)
2. Judgment at Poisoned Well (Pinnacle 1983)
3. Snake Eyes (Pinnacle 1984)
4. Dead Man's Hand (Pinnacle 1984)
5. River Race Verdict (Pinnacle 1984)
6. Shroud of Vengeance (Pinnacle 1985)
7. Old Bone Betrayal (Pinnacle 1985)
8. Teton Gamble (Pinnacle 1985)
9. Poison Bay (Pinnacle 1985)

97. DOOMSDAY MARSHAL
By Ray Hogan

John Rye is the Doomsday Marshal, assigned to bring law and order to the West. The paperback versions were issued by Signet.
The Doomsday Marshal (Doubleday 1975)
The Doomsday Posse (Doubleday 1977)
The Doomsday Trail (Doubleday 1979)
The Doomsday Bullet (Doubleday 1981)
The Doomsday Canyon (Doubleday 1984)

98. RONICKY DOONE
By David Manning
Frederick Faust penned these books.
Ronicky Doone (Chelsea House 1926)
Ronicky Doone's Treasure (Chelsea House 1926)

99. CORPORAL DOWNEY
By James B. Hendryx
The series features a Royal Canadian Mounted Policeman. The character also appears in Halfaday Creek stories by the same author.
Golden Girl (Putnam 1920) (Jarrolds 1923)
Downey of the Mounted (Putnam 1926) (Hutchinson 1926)
Blood on the Yukon Trail (Doubleday 1930) In the Days of Gold (Jarrolds 1930) Devil's Gold (Jarrolds 1940)
Corporal Downey Takes the Trail (Doubleday 1931) (Hutchinson 1932)
The Yukon Kid (Doubleday 1934) (Jarrolds 1934)
Blood of the North (Doubleday 1938) (Jarrolds 1938)

100. BUCK DUANE
By Zane Grey and Romer Zane Grey
In Zane Grey's original novel *Lone Star Ranger* (originally serialized in *All-Story*, reprinted in paper by Pocket), Buckley Duane, driven to becoming an outlaw, is pardoned through the efforts of Captain Jim MacNelly of the Texas Rangers. In the series of novelettes published in *Zane Grey's Western Magazine*, the character was continued under a house name. The Tower books were re-issued by Leisure in 1983-84. Another Zane Grey story about the character (last entry) was issued for the first time by the large-print publisher, with an introduction by Loren Grey.
Lone Star Ranger by Zane Grey (Harper & Row 1915)
Buck Duane: The Rider of Distant Trails by Romer Zane Grey (Belmont Tower 1980)
Buck Duane: King of the Range by Romer Zane Grey (Belmont Tower 1980) (Ian Henry 1986)
Three Deaths for Buck Duane (Ian Henry announced)
The Last of the Duanes by Zane Grey (John Curley & Associates 1983)

101. BUCK DUNNE
By G.J. Morgan
The series featuring a bounty hunter is written under a pseudonym by

Donald S. Rowland. The title below was announced as the first in a series.
Trail of Death (Future 1975)

102. EASTERN INDIAN SERIES
By Elmer Russell Gregor
This is a boys' book series.
Running Fox (D. Appleton 1918)
The White Wolf (D. Appleton 1921)
Spotted Deer (D. Appleton 1922)
The War Eagle (D. Appleton 1926)
The Spotted Pony (D. Appleton 1930)

103. EASY COMPANY
By John Wesley Howard
The series, likely written under a house name, relates the adventures of the members of a military outpost.
1. Easy Company and the Suicide Boys (Jove 1981)
2. Easy Company and the Medicine Gun (Jove 1981)
3. Easy Company and the Green Arrows (Jove 1981)
4. Easy Company and the White Man's Path (Jove 1981)
5. Easy Company and the Longhorns (Jove 1981)
6. Easy Company and the Big Medicine (Jove 1981)
7. Easy Company in the Black Hills (Jove 1981)
8. Easy Company on the Bitter Trail (Jove 1981)
9. Easy Company in Colter's Hell (Jove 1981)
10. Easy Company and the Headline Hunter Jove 1981)
11. Easy Company and the Engineers (Jove 1981)
12. Easy Company and the Bloody Flag (Jove 1982)
13. Easy Company on the Oklahoma Trail (Jove 1982)
14. Easy Company and the Cherokee Beauty (Jove 1982)
15. Easy Company and the Big Blizzard (Jove 1982)
16. Easy Company and the Long Marchers (Jove 1982)
17. Easy Company and the Bootleggers (Jove 1982)
18. Easy Company and the Card Sharps (Jove 1982)
19. Easy Company and the Indian Doctor (Jove 1982)
20. Easy Company and the Twilight Sniper (Jove 1982)
21. Easy Company and the Sheep Ranchers (Jove 1982)
22. Easy Company at Hat Creek Station (Jove 1982)
23. Easy Company and the Mystery Trooper (Jove 1982)
24. Easy Company and the Cow Country Queen (Jove 1983)
25. Easy Company and the Bible Salesman (Jove 1983)
26. Easy Comapny and the Blood Feud (Jove 1983)
27. Easy Company and the Dog Soldiers (Jove 1983)
28. Easy Company and the Big Name Hunter (Jove 1983)
29. Easy Company and the Gypsy Riders (Jove 1983)
30. Easy Company and the Bullwhackers (Jove 1983)
31. Easy Company and the Whiskey Trail (Jove 1983)

104. EDGE
By George G. Gilman

"Violence is a man! His name is Edge... The bloodiest action-series ever published, with a hero who is the meanest, most vicious killer the West has ever seen". That blurb from one of the books sums up this British series about Capt. Josiah C. Hedges written pseudonymously by Terry Harknett and others. See also next entry.
1. The Loner (New English Library 1972) (Pinnacle 1972)
2. Ten Thousand Dollars American (New English Library) Ten Grand (Pinnacle 1972)
3. Apache Death (New English Library 1972) (Pinnacle 1972)
4. Killer's Breed (New English Library 1972) (Pinnacle 1972)
5. Blood on Silver (New English Library 1972) (Pinnacle 1972)
6. The Blue, The Grey and The Red (New English Library 1973) Red River (Pinnacle 1973)
7. California Killing (New English Library 1973) California Kill (Pinnacle 1973)
8. Seven Out of Hell (New English Library 1973) Hell's Seven (Pinnacle 1973)
9. Bloody Summer (New English Library 1973) (Pinnacle 1974)
10. Vengeance is Black (New English Library 1973) Black Vengeance (Pinnacle 1974)
11. Sioux Uprising (New English Library 1974) (Pinnacle 1974)
12. The Biggest Bounty (New English Library 1974) Death's Bounty (Pinnacle 1974)
13. A Town Called Hate (New English Library 1974) The Hated (Pinnacle 1974)
14. The Big Gold (New English Library 1974) Tiger's Gold (Pinnacle 1974)
15. Blood Run (New English Library 1975) Paradise Loses (Pinnacle 1975)
16. The Final Shot (New English Library 1975) (Pinnacle 1975)
17. Vengeance Valley (New English Library 1975) (Pinnacle 1976)
18. Ten Tomstones to Texas (New English Library 1975) Ten Tombstones (Pinnacle 1976)
19. Ashes and Dust (New English Library 1976) (Pinnacle 1976)
20. Sullivan's Law (New English Library 1976) (Pinnacle 1976)
21. Rhapsody in Red (New English Library 1976) (Pinnacle 1977)
22. Slaughter Road (New English Library 1977) (Pinnacle 1977)
23. Echoes of War (New English Library 1977) (Pinnacle 1977)
24. The Day Democracy Died (New English Library 1977) Slaughterday (Pinnacle 1977)
25. Violence Trail (New English Library 1978) (Pinnacle 1978)
26. Savage Dawn (New English Library 1978) (Pinnacle 1978)
27. Death Drive (New English Library 1978) (Pinnacle 1978)
28. Eve of Evil (New English Library 1978) (Pinnacle 1978)
29. The Living, the Dying and the Dead (New English Library 1978) (Pinnacle 1979)

30. Waiting For a Train (New English Library 1979) Towering Nightmare (Pinnacle 1979)
31. Guilty Ones (New English Library 1979) (Pinnacle 1979)
32. Frightened Gun (New English Library 1979) (Pinnacle 1979)
33. The Hated (New English Library 1979) Red Fury (Pinnacle 1980)
34. A Ride in the Sun (New English Library 1980) (Pinnacle 1980)
35. Death Deal (New English Library 1980) (Pinnacle 1980)
36. Town on Trial (New English Library 1981) (Pinnacle 1980)
37. Vengeance at Ventura (New English Library 1981) (Pinnacle 1981)
38. Massacre Mission (New English Library 1981) (Pinnacle 1982)
39. The Prisoners (New English Library 1981) (Pinnacle 1982)
40. Montana Melodrama (New English Library 1982) (Pinnacle 1982)
41. The Killing Claim (New English Library 1982) (Pinnacle 1982)
42. Bloody Sunrise (New English Library) (Pinnacle 1983)
43. Arapaho Revenge (New English Library) (Pinnacle 1983)
44. The Blind Side (New English Library) (Pinnacle 1983)
45. House on the Range (New English Library) (Pinnacle 1983)
46. The Godforsaken (New English Library) (Pinnacle 1984)
47. The Moving Cage (New English Library) (Pinnacle 1985)
48. School for Slaughter (New English Library) (Pinnacle 1985)
49. Revenge Rider (New English Library) (Pinnacle 1985)

105. EDGE MEETS STEELE
By George G. Gilman
Two Gilman series heroes, Edge and Steel (see respective entries), were teamed for these books.
Two of a Kind: Edge Meets Steele (New English Library 1980) (Pinnacle 1980)
Matching Pair: Edge Meets Steele (New English Library 1982) (Pinnacle 1982)

106. BRECKINRIDGE ELKINS
By Robert E. Howard
Elkins, a hillbilly from the Nevada Humboldts, was featured in *Action Stories.*
A Gent from Bear Creek (Herbert Jenkins 1937) (Donald M. Grant 1965)
Pride of Bear Creek (Donald M. Grant 1966)
Mayhem on Bear Creek (Donald M. Grant 1979)
Heroes of Bear Creek (includes all three) (Ace 1983)

107. EMERALD CANYON
By Jeff Clinton
Jack M. Bickham used a pseudonym for this pair of novels about an impoverished young farmer in Arizona in the 1870s.
Emerald Canyon (Doubleday 1974)
Showdown at Emerald Canyon (Doubleday 1975)

108. THE EMIGRANTS
By Vilhelm Moberg
The four-part saga is about the Nillson family and its struggles in the New World. The novels, from the 1950s, are translated from the Swedish.
1. The Emigrants (Warner Books)
2. Unto a Good Land (Warner Books)
3. The Settlers (Warner Books)
4. Last Letter Home (Warner Books 1983)

DALE EVANS
See ROY ROGERS

109. FARGO
By John Benteen and John W. Hardin
Fargo was with Teddy Roosevelt's Rough Riders in Cuba, and frequently serves as a soldier of fortune in Mexico. Ben Haas wrote most of the early entries. *Sierra Silver* was published as by Hardin. The books appeared in Belmont Tower and Unibooks editions.
Fargo by John Benteen (Ben Haas) (Belmont Tower 1969)
Panama Gold by Benteen (Haas) (Belmont Tower 1970)
Massacre River by Benteen (Haas) (Belmont Tower 1970)
The Wildcatters by Benteen (Haas) (Belmont Tower 1970)
Alaska Gold by Benteen (Haas) (Belmont Tower 1970)
Apache Raiders by Benteen (Haas) (Belmont Tower 1970)
The Sharpshooter by Benteen (Haas) (Belmont Tower 1970)
Valley of Skulls by Benteen (Haas) (Belmont Tower 1970)
Wolf's Head by Benteen (Haas) (Belmont Tower 1970)
Killing Spree by Benteen (Haas) (Belmont Tower 1971)
The Black Bulls by Benteen (Haas) (Belmont Tower 1971)
Phantom Gunman by Bentéen (Haas) (Belmont Tower 1971)
Alaska Steel by Benteen (Belmont Tower)
Bandolero by Benteen (Belmont Tower)
Dynamite Fever by Benteen (Belmont Tower)
Gringo Guns by Benteen (Belmont Tower)
Shotgun Man by Benteen (Haas) (Belmont Tower 1973)
Sierra Silver by John W. Hardin (Belmont Tower 1974)
Hell on Wheels by Benteen (Haas) (Belmont Tower 1976)
Death Valley Gold by Benteen (Haas) (Belmont Tower 1976)
Border Jumpers by Benteen (Haas) (Belmont Tower 1976)
Killer's Moon by Benteen (Haas) (Belmont Tower 1976)
Dakota Badlands by Benteen (Haas) (Belmont Tower 1977)
Fargo and the Texas Rangers by Benteen (Haas) (Belmont Tower 1977)

FLAG AND FRONTIER SERIES
See FRONTIER SERIES

110. AMOS FLAGG
By Clay Randall
Clifton Adams penned these novels under the Randall byline. The series was originally issued by Fawcett, then re-issued as the Texas Lawman series by Belmont Tower. Atlantic Large Print re-issued the second book in 1983. Flagg is the sheriff in Academy, Texas. He is often at odds with his father, Gunner Flagg, a scruffy, bearded owlhoot who has spent some 20 years in prison.
 Amos Flagg — Lawman (Fawcett 1964)
 Amos Flagg — High Gun (Fawcett 1965)
 Amos Flagg — Bushwhacked (Fawcett 1967)
 Amos Flagg Has His Day (Fawcett 1968) The Killing of Billy Jowett (Belmont Tower)
 Amos Flagg Rides Out (Fawcett 1969)
 Amos Flagg — Showdown (Fawcett 1969)

111. FLOATING OUTFIT
By J.T. Edson
The prolific British author wrote this series for Brown, Watson and Corgi. Bantam and Berkley have reprinted the books in the United States. The main characters are a tough bunch of Rebels now working in Texas for Ole Devil Hardin's O.D. Connected ranch. They include Marc Counter, The Ysabel Kid, Belle Boyd, Dusty Fog, an ex-cavalryman now known as the Rio Hondo Gun Wizard, and Waco. (Hardin, Fog and Waco also have their own series.)
 Trail Boss (Brown, Watson 1961) (Berkley 1980)
 The Hard Riders (Brown, Watson 1962) (Berkley 1986)
 The Texan (Brown, Watson 1962) (Berkley)
 Rio Guns (Brown, Watson 1962) (Berkley 1983)
 The Ysabel Kid (Brown, Watson 1962) (Berkley 1978)
 Quiet Town (as Chuck Nolan) (Brown, Watson 1962) (as J.T. Edson) (Berkley 1980)
 Waco's Debt (Brown, Watson 1962) (Berkley 1986)
 The Rio Hondo Kid (Brown, Watson 1963) (Berkley 1983)
 Apache Rampage (Brown, Watson 1963) (Berkley 1984)
 The Half Breed (Brown, Watson 1963) (Berkley 1981)
 Gun Wizard (Brown, Watson 1963) (Berkley 1983)
 Gunsmoke Thunder (Brown, Watson 1963) (Berkley 1985)
 Wagons to Backsight (Brown, Watson 1964) (Berkley 1980)
 The Rushers (Brown, Watson 1964) (Berkley)
 The Rio Hondo War (Brown, Watson 1964) (Berkley 1984)
 Trigger Fast (Brown, Watson 1964) (Berkley 1983)
 The Wildcats (Brown, Watson 1965) (Berkley 1981)
 The Peacemakers (Brown, Watson 1965) (Berkley 1982)
 Troubled Range (Brown, Watson 1965) (Berkley 1979)
 The Fortune Hunters (Brown, Watson 1965) (Berkey)
 The Man from Texas (Brown, Watson 1965) (Berkley 1984)
 The Trouble Busters (Brown, Watson 1965) (Berkley)

Guns in the Night (Brown, Watson 1966) (Berkley 1985)
A Town Called Yellowdog (Brown, Watson 1966) (Berkley 1981)
The Law of the Gun (Brown, Watson 1966) (Berkley 1982)
Return to Backsight (Brown, Watson 1966) (Berkley)
The Fast Guns (Brown, Watson 1967) (Berkley 1981)
Terror Valley (Brown, Watson 1967) (Berkley 1984)
Sidewinder (Brown, Watson 1967) (Berkley 1979)
The Floating Outfit (Corgi 1968) (Berkley 1984)
The Bad Bunch (Corgi 1968) (Berkley 1979)
The Hooded Riders (Corgi 1968) (Berkley 1980)
Rangeland Hercules (Corgi 1968) (Berkley 1981)
McGraw's Inheritance (Corgi 1968) (Berkley 1979)
The Making of a Lawman (Corgi 1968) (Bantam 1971) (Berkley)
The Town Tamers (Corgi 1969) (Bantam 1973)
The Small Texan (Corgi 1969) (Bantam 1974) (Berkley 1985)
Cuchilo (Corgi 1969) (Berkley 1981)
Goodnight's Dream (Corgi 1969) (Berkley 1980) The Floating Outfit
(Bantam 1974)
From Hide and Horn (Corgi 1969) (Bantam 1974) (Berkley 1980)
.44 Calibre Man (Corgi 1969) (Bantam 1974) (Berkley)
A Horse Called Mogollon (Corgi 1971) (Berkley 1980)
Hell in the Palo Duro (Corgi 1971) (Berkley 1979)
Go Back to Hell (Corgi 1972) (Berkley 1979)
The South Will Rise Again (Corgi 1972) (Berkley 1980)
To Arms, To Arms, in Dixie (Corgi 1972) (Berkley 1980)
Set Texas Back on Her Feet (Corgi 1973) (Berkley 1986) Viridian's
Trail (Berkley 1979)
The Hide and Tallow Man (Corgi 1974) (Berkley 1978)
The Quest for Bowie's Blade (Corgi 1974) (Berkley)
Set A-Foot (Corgi 1978)
Beguinage (Corgie 1978)
Beguinage is Dead! (Corgi 1978)
Renegade (Berkley 1978)
The Gentle Giant (Corgi 1979) (Berkley 1986)
Master of Triggernometry (Corgi 1981)
White Indian (Corgi 1981) (Berkley 1985)
Old Mocassins on the Trail (Corgi 1981) (Berkley 1985)

112. CAP FOG
By J.T. Edson
This character also appears in other of the author's series.
Cap Fog, Meet Mr. J.G. Reeder (Corgi 1977)
You're a Texas Ranger, Alvin Fog (Corgi 1979)
Rapido Clint (Corgi 1980)
The Justice of Company Z (Corgi 1981)

113. FOXX
By Zack Tyler

Foxx is chief detective for the California & Kansas Railroad in this adult series copyright by Mel Marshall.
1. Foxx (Dell 1981)
2. Foxx's Gold (Dell 1981)
3. Foxx Hunting (Dell 1981)
4. Foxx's Herd (Dell 1981)
5. Foxx's Foe (Dell 1982)

114. FRENCH AND INDIAN WAR SERIES
By Joseph A. Altsheler
This is a boys' book series.
The Hunters of the Hills (D. Appleton 1916)
The Shadow of the North (D. Appleton 1917)
The Rulers of the Lakes (D. Appleton 1917)
The Masters of the Peaks (D. Appleton 1918)
The Lords of the Wild (D. Appleton 1919)
The Sun of Quebec (D. Appleton 1919)

115. THE FRONTIER SERIES
By Capt. Ralph Bonehill
These are Stratemeyer Syndicate boys' books. The fourth through ninth entries were added and the series was re-titled Flag and Frontier Series when issued by Grosset & Dunlap.
With Boone on the Frontier or, The Pioneer Boys of Old Kentucky (Mershon 1903)
Pioneer Boys of the Great Northwest or, With Lewis and Clark Across the Rockies (Merson 1904)
Pioneer Boys of the Goldfields or, The Nugget Hunters of '49 (Merson 1906)
With Custer in the Black Hills or, A Young Scout Among the Indians (Grosset & Dunlap 1902)
Boys of the Fort or, A Young Captain's Pluck (Grosset & Dunlap 1901)
The Young Bandmaster or, Concert Stage and Battlefield (Grosset & Dunlap 1900)
Off for Hawaii or, The Mystery of a Great Volcano (Grosset & Dunlap 1899)
A Sailor Boy with Dewey or, Afloat in the Phillipines (Grosset & Dunlap 1899)
When Santiago Fell or, The War Adventures of Two Chums (Grosset & Dunlap 1899)

116. THE FRONTIER BOYS
By Capt. Wyn Roosevelt
This is a boys' book series.
The Frontier Boys on Overland Trail or, Across the Plains of Kansas (A.L. Chatterton 1908)
The Frontier Boys in Colorado or, Captured by Indians (A.L. Chatterton 1908)

The Frontier Boys in the Rockies or, Lost in the Mountains (A.L. Chatterton 1909)
The Frontier Boys in the Grand Canyon or, A Search for Treasure (A.L. Chatterton 1908)
The Frontier Boys in Mexico or, Mystery Mountain (A.L. Chatterton 1908)
The Frontier Boys on the Coast or, In the Pirate's Power (A.L. Chatterton 1909)
The Frontier Boys in Hawaii or, The Mystery of the Hollow Mountain (A.L Chatterton 1909)
The Frontier Boys in the Sierras or, The Lost Mine (A.L Chatterton 1909)
The Frontier Boys in the Saddle (A.L. Chatterton 1910)
The Frontier Boys in Frisco (A.L. Chatterton 1911)
The Frontier Boys in the South Seas (A.L. Chatterton 1912)

117. THE FRONTIER RAKERS
By David Norman
The saga depicts the exploits of Western travelers on a wagon train, in a mining camp, etc.
1. The Frontier Rakers (Zebra 1981)
2. The Forty-Niners (Zebra 1981)
3. Gold Fever (Zebra 1981)
4. Silver City (Zebra 1982)
5. Montana Pass (Zebra 1982)
6. Santa Fe Dream (Zebra 1983)

118. FRONTIER GIRL
By Alice Turner Curtis
This is a girls' book series.
A Frontier Girl of Virginia (Penn 1929)
A Frontier Girl of Massachusetts (Penn 1930)
A Frontier Girl of New York (Penn 1931)
A Frontier Girl of Chesapeake Bay (Penn 1934)
A Frontier Girl of Pennzylvania (Penn 1937)

119. FRONTIER WOMEN
By Kitt Brown and Jeanne Foster
This saga series is about women in the West.
1. Kentucky Spitfire — Caitlyn McGregor by Kitt Brown (Fawcett 1981)
2. Missouri Flame — Deborah Leigh by Jeanne Foster (Fawcett 1981)
3. Texas Wildflower — Laurian Kane by Brown (Fawcett 1982)
4. Wyoming Glory — Eden Richards by Foster (Fawcett 1982)

120. FURY
By Albert G. Miller
The black horse, his young master Joey and the Broken Wheel Ranch

were featured in a television program 1955-66.
1. Fury, Stallion of Broken Wheel Ranch (Grosset & Dunlap)
2. Fury and the Mustangs (Grosset & Dunlap 1960)
3. Fury and the White Mare (Grosset & Dunlap)

121. GLENGARRY
By Ralph Connor
Charles William Gordon wrote these books about western Canada.
  The Man from Glengarry (Westminster 1901) (Revell 1901)
  Glengarry School Days: A Story of Early Days in Glengarry
(Westminster 1902) (Revell 1902) Glengarry Days (Hodder & Stoughton
1902)
  The Girl from Glengarry (McClelland and Stewart 1933) (Dodd, Mead
1933) The Glengarry Girl (Lane 1934).
  Torches Through the Bush: A Tale of Glengarry (McClelland and
Stewart 1934) (Dodd, Mead 1934) (Lane 1935)

122. GOLD
By Clay Turner
Ben Gold is a Jewish storekeeper, Indian fighter, horseman and expert
with gun and dice. W.T. Ballard wrote the books.
  Give A Man A Gun (Warner Paperback Library 1971)
  Go West, Ben Gold (Warner Paperback Library 1974)
  Gold Goes to the Mountain (Warner Paperback Library 1974)

GOLD MAN
  See JIM STEEL

123. ROSS GRANT SERIES
By John Garland
This is a boys' book series.
  Ross Grant, Tenderfoot (Penn 1915)
  Ross Grant, Gold Hunter (Penn 1916)
  Ross Grant on the Trail (Penn 1917)
  Ross Grant in Miner's Camp (Penn 1918)

124. GREAT AMERICAN INDIAN CHIEFS
By E.T. Tomlinson and Paul G. Tomlinson
This is a boys' book series.
  The Trail of Black Hawk by E.T. Tomlinson (D. Appleton 1915)
  The Trail of the Mohawk Chief by E.T. Tomlinson (D. Appleton 1916)
  The Trail of Tecumseh by Paul G. Tomlinson (D. Appleton 1917)

125. GREAT INDIAN WARRIORS
By Will Henry
Bantam in the 1980s grouped a number of the author's Indian novels
together under the banner Great Indian Warriors. The writer is actually
Henry Wilson Allen.

Maheo's Children (Chilton 1968) The Squaw Killers (Bantam 1971)
No Survivors (Random House 1950)
Pillars of the Sky (Bantam 1956)
One More River to Cross (Random House 1967)
The Day Fort Larking Fell (Chilton 1969)

126. GREAT WEST
By Joseph A. Altsheler
This is a boys' book series.
The Great Sioux Trail (D. Appleton 1918)
The Lost Hunters (D. Appleton 1918)

127. GRIMSEN TRILOGY
By Sophus K. Winther
These books are about a Danish immigrant family.
Take All to Nebraska (Macmillan 1935)
Mortgage Your Heart (Macmillan 1937)
This Passion Never Dies (Macmillan 1938)

128. GRINGOS
By J.D. Sandon
The British series is about four men thrown together during the Mexican
Revolution: Cade Onslow, Jonas Strong, Jamie Durham and Yates Mc-
Cloud.
1. Guns Across the River (Granada 1979)
2. Cannons in the Rain (by John B. Harvey) (Granada 1979)
3. Fire in the Wind (Granada 1979))
4. Border Affair (by Harvey) (Granada 1979)
5.
6. Mazatlan (by Harvey) (Granada 1980)
7.
8. Wheels of Thunder (by Harvey) (Granada 1981)

129. EDEN GROVE
By Dwight Bennett
Dwight Bennett Newton wrote these books.
West of Railhead (Doubleday 1977)
The Texans (Doubleday 1979)

130. GUN LUST
By W.L. Fieldhouse
Shaddrock and Cougar are good at "Chasing bad men and good
women," according to a cover blurb for this adult series.
1. Gun Lust (Leisure 1982)
2. Gun Lust: Comanchero Kill (Leisure 1983)

131. GUNN
By Jory Sherman

Gunn is a stud cowboy in this adult series.
1. Dawn of Revenge (Zebra 1980)
2. Mexican Showdown (Zebra 1980)
3. Death's Head Trail (Zebra 1980)
4. Blood Justice (Zebra 1980)
5. Winter Hell (Zebra 1981)
6. Duel in Purgatory (Zebra 1981)
7. Law of the Rope (Zebra 1981)
8. Apache Arrows (Zebra 1981)
9. Boothill Bounty (Zebra 1981)
10. Hard Bullets (Zebra 1981)
11. Trial by Sixgun (Zebra 1981)
12. The Widow Maker (Zebra 1982)
13. Arizona Hardcase (Zebra 1982)
14. The Buff Runners (Zebra 1982)
15. Drygulched (Zebra 1982)
16. Wyoming Wanton (Zebra 1982)
17. Tucson Twosome (Zebra 1983)
18. The Golden Lady (Zebra 1983)
19. High Mountain Hussey (Zebra 1984)
20. Ten-Gallon Tease (Zebra 1984)
21. Sweet Texas Tart (Zebra 1984)
22. Kansas Kitten (Zebra 1985)
23. Bedroll Beauty (Zebra 1985)
24. Frontier Fanny (Zebra 1986)

132. THE GUNSMITH
By J.R. Roberts
Clint Adams, the Gunsmith, is featured in this adult cowboy series by
Robert J. Randisi.
1. Maclin's Women (Ace Charter 1982)
2. The Chinese Gunmen (Ace Charter 1982)
3. The Woman Hunt (Ace Charter 1982)
4. The Guns of Abilene (Ace Charter 1982)
5. Three Guns for Glory (Ace Charter 1982)
6. Leadtown (Ace Charter 1982)
7. The Longhorn War (Ace Charter 1982)
8. Quanah's Revenge (Ace Charter 1982)
9. Heavyweight Gun (Ace Charter 1982)
10. New Orleans Fire (Ace Charter 1982)
11. One-Handed Gun (Ace Charter 1982)
12. The Canadian Payroll (Ace Charter 1983)
13. Draw to an Inside Death (Ace Charter 1983)
14. Dead Man's Hand (Ace Charter 1983)
15. Bandit Gold (Ace Charter 1983)
16. Buckskins and Sixguns (Ace Charter 1983)
17. Silver War (Ace Charter 1983)
18. High Noon at Lancaster (Ace Charter 1983)

19. Bandido Blood (Ace Charter 1983)
20. The Dodge City Gang (Ace Charter 1983)
21. Sasquatch Hunt (Ace Charter 1983)
22. Bullets and Ballots (Ace Charter 1983)
23. The Riverboat Gang (Ace Charter 1983)
24. Killer Grizzley (Ace Charter 1984)
25. North of the Border (Ace Charter 1984)
26. Eagle's Gap (Ace Charter 1984)
27. Chinatown Hell (Ace Charter 1984)
28. The Panhandle Search (Ace Charter 1984)
29. Wildcat Roundup (Ace Charter 1984)
30. The Ponderosa War (Ace Charter 1984)
31. Trouble Rides a Fast Horse (Ace Charter 1984)
32. Dynamite Justice (Ace Charter 1984)
33. The Posse (Ace Charter 1984)
34. Night of the Gila (Ace Charter 1984)
35. The Bounty Women (Ace Charter 1984)
36. Black Pearl Saloon (Ace Charter 1985)
37. Gundown in Paradise (Ace Charter 1985)
38. King of the Border (Ace Charter 1985)
39. The El Paso Salt War (Ace Charter 1985)
40. The Ten Pines Killer (Ace Charter 1985)
41. Hell With A Pistol (Ace Charter 1985)
42. Wyoming Cattle Kill (Ace Charter 1985)
43. The Golden Horseman (Ace Charter 1985)
44. The Scarlet Gun (Ace Charter 1985)
45. Navaho Devil (Ace Charter 1985)
46. Wild Bill's Ghost (Ace Charter 1985)
47. The Miner's Showdown (Ace Charter 1985)
48. Archer's Revenge (Ace Charter 1986)
49. Showdown in Raton (Ace Charter 1986)
50. When Legends Meet (Ace Charter 1986)
51. Desert Hell (Ace Charter 1986)
52. The Diamond Run (Ace Charter 1986)
53. Denver Duo (Ace Charter 1986)

133. GUNSMOKE
By Various Authors
This series is based on the long-running (1955-75) television program about Marshal Matt Dillon of Dodge City, Kansas.
1. The Renegades by John Flynn (Award)
2. Shootout by Gordon D. Shirreffs (Award 1974)
3. Duel at Dodge City by Flynn (Award 1974)
4. Cheyenne Vengeance by Flynn (Award)
Gunsmoke by Robert Turner (Whitman 1958)
Gunsmoke: Showdown on Front Street by Paul S. Newman (Winston 1969)
Gunsmoke by Chris Stratton (Popular Library 1970)

134. HALFADAY CREEK
By James B. Hendryx
The series is set on the Yukon-Alaska border. The main characters are Black John Smith and Lyme Cushing, proprietor of Cushing's Fort, a bar and store in remote mining country. Corporal Downey, who has his own series, also often appears. Many of the Halfaday Creek books originally appeared as pulp magazine novelettes.
  Outlaws of Halfaday Creek (Doubleday 1935) (Jarrolds 1935)
  Black John of Halfaday Creek (Doubleday 1938) (Jarrolds 1939)
  The Czar of Halfaday Creek (Doubleday 1940) (Jarrolds 1955)
  Law and Order on Halfaday Creek (Carlton House 1941) (Jarrolds 1954)
  Gold and Guns on Halfaday Creek (Carlton House 1943) (Hale 1953)
  Strange Doings on Halfaday Creek (Doubleday 1943) (Hale 1952)
  It Happened On Halfaday Creek (Doubleday 1944)
  Skullduggery on Halfaday Creek (Doubleday 1946) (Hammond 1953)
  The Saga of Halfaday Creek (Doubleday 1947) (Hammond 1954)
  Justice on Halfaday Creek (Doubleday 1949) (Museum Press 1954)
  Badmen on Halfaday Creek (Doubleday 1950) (Hammond 1956)
  Murder on Halfaday Creek (Doubleday 1951)
  Intrigue on Halfaday Creek (Doubleday 1953)
  Terror on Halfaday Creek (Consul 1963)

135. DAVE HALLORAN
By Lee Denver
This is a British series.
  Trail to Maverick (Hale 1965)
  Pay Off For Wells Fargo (Hale 1967)
  Showdown at Sandy Gulch (Hale 1968)

136. OLE DEVIL HARDIN
By J.T. Edson
Hardin owns the O.D. Connected Ranch, for which the Floating Outfit (see that series) works.
  Young Ole Devil (Corgi 1975)
  Get Urrea (Corgi 1975)
  Ole Devil and the Caplocks (Corgi 1976)
  Ole Devil and the Mule Train (Corgi 1976)
  Ole Devil at San Jacinto (Corgi 1977)

137. THE GRACE HARLOWE OVERLAND RIDERS SERIES
By Josephine Chase
Jessie Graham Flower wrote this girls' book series
  Grace Harlowe's Overland Riders Among the Kentucky Mountains (Saalfield 1921)
  Grace Harlowe's Overland Riders in the Great North Woods (Altemus 1921)
  Grace Harlowe's Overland Riders on the Great American Desert

(Altemus 1921)
Grace Harlowe's Overland Riders on the Old Apache Trail (Altemus 1921)
Grace Harlowe's Overland Riders at Circle O Ranch (Altemus 1923)
Grace Harlowe's Overland Riders in the Black Hills (Altemus 1923)
Grace Harlowe's Overland Riders in the High Sierras (Altemus 1923)
Grace Harlowe's Overland Riders in the Yellowstone National Park (Altemus 1923)
Grace Harlowe's Overland Rider Among the Border Guerillas (Altemus 1924)
Grace Harlowe's Overland Riders on the Lost River Trail (Altemus 1924)

138. HART THE REGULATOR
By John B. Harvey
This is a British series.
1. Cherokee Outlet (Pan 1980)
2. Blood Trail (Pan 1980)
3. Tago (Pan 1980)
4. The Silver Lie (Pan 1980)
5. Blood on the Border (Pan 1981)
6. Ride the Wide Country (Pan 1981)

139. HASHKNIFE HARTLEY
By W.C. Tuttle
Hashknife Hartley and his saddle pard Sleepy Stevens frequently work undercover as rangeland detectives for the Cattlemen's Association. The duo appeared in hardcover books and pulp magazines before being reprinted in paperback.
The Medicine Man (Collins 1925) (Houghton Mifflin 1939)
Hashknife Lends a Hand (Collins 1927)
Thicker Than Water (Houghton Mifflin 1927)
Shotgun Gold (Houghton Mifflin 1927)
The Morgan Trail (Houghton Mifflin 1928)
Hashknife of the Canyon Trail (Collins 1928)
Hashknife of the Double Bar S (Houghton Mifflin 1936) (Collins 1929)
Arizona Ways (Collins 1929)
Tumbling River Range (Collins 1929) (Houghton Mifflin 1935)
Hashknife of Stormy River (Collins 1931) (Houghton Mifflin 1935)
The Santa Dolores Stage (Houghton Mifflin 1934) Twisted Trails (Popular Library 1949)
Rifled Gold (Houghton Mifflin 1934) (Collins 1934)
Ghost Trails (Houghton Mifflin 1940)
Valley of Vanishing Herds (Houghton Mifflin 1942)
The Trouble Trailer (Houghton Mifflin 1946)
Hidden Blood (Popular Library 1948)

140. FANCY HATCH
By Zachary Hawkes
Fancy Hatch, "A hundred and ten pounds of beautiful trouble," is a female deputy sheriff in this adult series by Alan Riefe.
1. Fancy Hatch (Pinnacle Crossfire 1984)
2. The Case Deuce (Pinnacle Crossfire 1984)
3. Solomon King's Mine (Pinnacle Crossfire 1984)
4. The Odds Against Sundown (Pinnacle Crossfire 1985)

141. RANGER JIM HATFIELD (I)
By Jackson Cole
This series reprinted adventures from the pulp *Texas Rangers*, which ran from 1938 to the mid-1950s. The stories were written mostly by, alternately, Tom Curry and A. Leslie. Curry also penned entries in the Rio Kid seriers. Leslie later wrote another ranger series under the Bradford Scott penname. Hatfield is also known by the nickname Lone Wolf, and his horse is called Goldie.
   The Tombstone Trail (Popular 1967)
   Kiowa Killer (Popular 1967)
   The Vanishing Vaqueros (Popular 1967)
   Brand of the Lawless (Popular 1968)
   The Frontier Legion (Popular 1968)
   Gun Harvest (Popular 1968)
   Guns of El Gato (Popular 1968)
   The Hell-Benders (Popular 1968)
   Range of No Return (Popular 1968)
   Texas Trigger (Popular 1968)
   Outlaw Empire (Popular 1968)
   Badman's Range (Popular 1969)
   Drygulchers (Popular 1969)
   Fast Draw (Popular 1969)
   Bullets on the Border (Popular 1969)
   Gunslinger's Range (Popular 1969)
   Guns of Vengeance (Popular 1969)
   Red River Showdown (Popular 1969)
   Six-Gun Fury (Popular 1969)
   Trouble on Trinity Range (Popular 1969)
   Trail Town Guns (Popular 1969)
   Outlaws of the Big Bend (Popular 1969)
   Badmen of Bordertown (Popular 1970)
   The Black Hat Riders (Popular 1970)
   Dead Man's Canyon (Popular 1970)
   Free Range (Popular 1970)
   Outlaw Valley (Popular 1970)
   Two Guns for Texas (Popular 1970)
   West of the Pecos (Popular 1970)
   Six-Gun Syndicate (Popular 1970)
   Six-Gun Hills (Popular 1970)

Texas Showdown (Popular 1970)
Gunfire Land (Popular 1971)
Gun-Down on the Rio (Popular 1971)
Hell in Paradise (Popular 1971)
Outlaw Hell (Popular 1971)
Pecos Poison (Popular 1971)
Shootout Trail (Popular 1971)
Trouble Range (Popular 1971)
Power of the Range (Popular 1971)
Six-Gun Country (Popular 1972)
Riders of the Shadows (Popular 1972)
Red Runs the Rio (Popular 1972)
The Red Marauders (Popular 1972)
Panhandle Bandits (Popular 1972)
Mesquite Marauders (Popular 1972)
Lone Star Peril (Popular 1972)
Death Rides the Rio (Popular 1972)
Guns Across the Pecos (Popular 1972)
The Brass Circle (Popular 1973)
Gunsmoke Empire (Popular 1973)
Riders of the Mesquite Trail (Popular 1973)
Vaquero Guns (Popular 1973)
Peril Rides the Pecos (Popular 1973)
The Riders (Popular 1974)
The Lobo Legion (Popular 1974)
Bayou Guns (Popular 1974)
Death Rides the Star Route (Popular 1974)
Dinero of Doom (Popular 1975)
Guns of Fort Griffin (Popular 1975)
Lobo Colonel (Popular 1975)
Lost River Loot (Popular 1975)
The Skeleton Riders (Popular 1975)
Tin-Star Target (Popular 1975)
The Land Pirates (Popular 1976)
Bugles on the Bighorn (Popular 1976)
Crown for Azora (Popular 1976)
On to Cheyenne (Popular 1976)
Passport to Perdition (Popular 1976)
Raiders of the Valley (Popular 1976)
Sante Fe Trail (Popular 1976)
Trail of the Iron Horse (Popular 1976)
Gun Fight at Deep River (Popular)
White Gold of Texas (Popular)

142. RANGER JIM HATFIELD (II)
By Jackson Cole
Before the pulp magazine *Texas Rangers* had run its course, the main

character was given a series of original books from Pyramid. A. Leslie Scott wrote the entries. The books were re-issued in the early 1960s.

Guns of Mist River (Pyramid 1950)
Texas Fury (Pyramid 1951)
Thunder Range (Pyramid 1952)
Border Hell (Pyramid 1952)
The Death Riders (Pyramid 1952)
Trigger Law (Pyramid 1952)
Massacre Canyon (Pyramid 1953)
Killer Country (Pyramid 1953)
Texas Fists (Pyramid 1953)
Gun-Runners (Pyramid 1953)
Land Grab (Pyramid 1953)
Texas Tornado (Pyramid 1954)
Guntown (Pyramid 1954)
Outlawed (Pyramid 1954)
Bullets High (Pyramid 1954)
Texas Manhunt (Pyramid 1955)
Gunsmoke Trail (Pyramid 1955)
Trouble Shooter (Pyramid 1955)
Gun Blaze (Pyramid 1955)
Two-Gun Devil (Pyramid 1955)

143. HAVE GUN, WILL TRAVEL
By Various Authors
Many of television's popular Western programs of the 1950s and '60s spawned paperback books (though not necessarily series), among them "Rawhide," "Wanted: Dead or Alive," "Tales of Wells Fargo," "Cheyenne," "F-Troop" and "The Big Valley." Paladin, the hero of "Have Gun, Will Travel" (which aired 1957-63), is a gentleman and gunman for hire.

Have Gun, Will Travel (Whitman 1959)
Have Gun, Will Travel by Noel Loomis (Dell 1960)
A Man Called Paladin by Frank G. Robertson (McFadden Books 1964)

HAWK
See SAGA OF THE SOUTHWEST

144. HAWK (I)
By William S. Brady
This is a British cowboy series.
1.
2. Blood Money (by John B. Harvey) (Fontana 1979)
3.
4. Killing Time (by Harvey) (Fontana 1980)
5.
6. Blood Kin (by Harvey) (Fontana 1980)
7.
8. Desperadoes (by Harvey) (Fontana 1981)

9.
10. Dead Man's Gold (by Harvey) (Fontana 1981)
11. Sierra Gold (by Harvey) (Fontana 1981)

145. HAWK (II)
By Brett Sanders
Web Steele, alias Hawk, is a gunman.
1. Hawk (Award 1974)
2. Vengeance Gun (Award 1974)
3. Blood Bait (Award 1974)
4. Shootout at Las Cruces (Award 1976)

HAWKEYE
See DEERSLAYER

146. HERNE THE HUNTER
By John J. McLaglen
This is a British series written by John B. Harvey and others.
1.
2. River of Blood (by John B. Harvey) (Corgi 1976)
3.
4. Shadow of the Vulture (by Harvey) (Corgi 1977)
5.
6. Death in Gold (by Harvey) (Corgi 1977)
7.
8. Cross-Draw (by Harvey) (Corgi 1978)
9.
10. Vigilante! (by Harvey) (Corgi 1979)
11.
12. Sun Dance (by Harvey) (Corgi 1980)
13. Billy the Kid (by Harvey) (Corgi 1980)
14.
15. Till Death... (by Harvey) (Corgi 1980)

147. JEFFERSON HEWITT
By John Reese
The frontier detective appeared in a series of hardcover books, some of which were reprinted in paperback by Belmont Tower and Leisure.
Weapon Heavy (Doubleday 1973)
They Don't Shoot Cowards (Doubleday 1973)
Texas Gold (Doubleday 1975)
Wes Hardin's Gun (Doubleday 1975)
The Sharpshooter (Doubleday 1975)
Hangman's Springs (Doubleday 1976)
Sequois Shootout (Doubleday 1977)
The Cherokee Diamondback (Doubleday 1977)
Dead Eye (Doubleday 1978)
Two Thieves and a Puma (Doubleday 1980)

148. THE HIGH CHAPARREL
By Various Authors
The 1967-71 television seies about the Cannon and Montoya ranches in Arizona Territory spurred this series.
Hell and High Water by Wayne Sotona (Tempo 1968)
Coyote Gold By Ed Friend (Tempo 1968)
Apache Way by Steve Frazee (Whitman 1969)

149. RUSTY HINES
By Arthur Nickson
This is a British series.
Rusty Hines Hits the Trail (Jenkins 1958)
Rusty Hines — Trouble Shooter (Jenkins 1959)

HOW THE WEST REALLY WAS
See ANGEL

BURN HUDNALL
See YAQUI

150. BILL HUNTER
By David Manning
Frederick Faust wrote these books.
Bill Hunter (Chelsea House 1924)
Bill Hunter's Romance (Chelsea House 1924)

151. VRIDAR HUNTER TRILOGY
By Vardis Fisher
A rugged wilderness figures in the writer's works.
In Tragic Life (Caxton 1932) I See No Sin (Boriswood 1934)
Passions Spin the Plot (Doubleday 1934) (Boriswood 1935)
We Are Betrayed (Doubleday 1936) (Boriswood 1936)
No Villain Need Be (Doubleday 1937)

152. IMMIGRANT TRILOGY
By O.E. Rolvaag
The Norwegian-American author wrote three books about an immigrant family in America.
Giants in the Earth (Harper's 1927) (Benn 1927)
Peder Victorious (Harper's 1929)
Their Father's God (Harper's 1931)

153. INDIAN SERIES
By James Braden
This is a boys' book series.
Far Past the Frontier (Saalfield 1902)
The Lone Indian (Saalfield 1903)
The Trail of the Seneca (Saalfield 1907)

154. INDIAN ECSTACY
By Janelle Taylor
Elisha loves Grey Eagle in this romantic Western series.
Savage Ecstacy (Zebra 1981)
Defiant Ecstacy (Zebra 1982)
Forbidden Ecstacy (Zebra 1982)
Brazen Ecstacy (Zebra 1983)
Tender Ecstacy (Zebra 1983)
Stolen Ecstacy (Zebra 1985)

155. INDIAN HERITAGE
By Paul Joseph Lederer
This epic series is about Indians.
1. Manitou's Daughter (Signet 1982)
2. Shawnee Dawn (Signet 1983)
3. Seminole Skies (Signet 1983)
4. Cheyenne Dream (Signet 1985)
5. The Way of the Wind (Signet 1986)

156. INDIAN STORIES
By Dietrich Lange
This is a boys' book series.
On the Trail of the Sioux (Lathrop, Lee and Shepard 1912)
The Silver Island of the Chippewa (Lathrop, Lee and Shepard 1913)
Lost in the Fur Country (Lathrop, Lee and Shepard 1914)
In the Great Wild North (Lathrop, Lee and Shepard 1915)
The Lure of the Black Hills (Lathrop, Lee and Shepard 1916)
The Lure of the Mississippi (Lathrop, Lee and Shepard 1917)
The Silver Cache of the Pawnees (Lathrop, Lee and Shepard 1918)
The Shawnee's Warning (Lathrop, Lee and Shepard 1919)
The Threat of Sitting Bull (Lathrop, Lee and Shepard 1920)
The Raid of the Ottawa (Lathrop, Lee and Shepard 1921)
The Mohawk Ranger (Lathrop, Lee and Shepard 1922)
The Iroquois Scout (Lathrop, Lee and Shepard 1923)
The Sioux Runner (Lathrop, Lee and Shepard 1924)
The Gold Rock of the Chippewa (Lathrop, Lee and Shepard 1925)
The Boast of the Seminole (Lathrop, Lee and Shepard 1930)
On the Fur Trail (Lathrop, Lee and Shepard 1931)

157. INDIAN STORIES FOR BOYS
By H.L. Risteen
This is a boys' book series.
Chippeway Captive (Cupples and Leon 1948)
Indian Silver (Cupples and Leon 1948)
Tomahawk Trail (Cupples and Leon 1948)
Black Hawk's Warpath (Cupples and Leon 1950)
Redskin Raiders (Cupples and Leon 1951)
Montana Gold (Cupples and Leon 1951)

JAMES BOYS
  See BUFFALO BILL

158. ARVADA JONES
  By Les Wayne
Jones, once a trapper happily married to a young Cheyenne woman, has taken to wandering since the death of his wife and young son. Some of the books have been reprinted by John Curley & Associates in large-print editions.
  West of Omaha (Leisure 1981)
  Cheyenne Manhunt (Leisure 1981)
  Warpaint (Leisure 1982)
  Arvada Jones and the Orphans of the Trail (Leisure 1982)

159. CHEYENNE JONES
  By Lee Denver
This is a British series.
  Cheyenne Swings a Wide Loop (Mayflower 1971)
  The Gun Code of Cheyenne Jones (Mayflower 1971)
  Three Slugs for Cheyenne (Hale 1971)
  Cheyenne Pays in Lead (Hale 1972)
  Lone Trail for Cheyenne (Hale 1973)
  Cheyenne Bucks the Law (Hale 1975)
  Cheyenne Jones, Maverick Marshal (Hale 1977)
  Cheyenne's Sixgun Justice (Hale 1980)

160. WYOMING JONES
  By Richard Telfair
Jones is a range-riding cowboy in this series by Richard Jessup.
  Wyoming Jones (Fawcett 1958)
  Day of the Gun (Fawcett 1958)
  Wyoming Jones for Hire (Fawcett 1958)

161. JORY
  By Milton R. Bass
The first of these two novels about the coming of age of young Jory was made into a film in 1972 with Robby Benson in the title role.
  Jory (G.P. Putnam's Sons 1969)
  Mistr Jory (G.P. Putnam's Sons 1976)

JUSTICE SERIES
  See ANGEL

162. RUFF JUSTICE
  By Warren T. Longtree
Justice is a frontier scout and adventurer in this apparently pseudonymous adult series.
  1. Sudden Thunder (Signet 1981)

2. Night of the Apache (Signet 1981)
3. Blood on the Moon (Signet 1981)
4. Widow Creek (Signet 1982)
5. Valley of Golden Tombs (Signet 1982)
6. The Spirit Woman War (Signet 1982)
7. Dark Angel Riding (Signet 1982)
8. The Death of Iron Horse (Signet 1983)
9. Windwolf (Signet 1983)
10. Shoshone Run (Signet 1983)
11. Comanche Peak (Signet 1983)
12. Petticoat Express (Signet 1984)
13. Power Lode (Signet 1984)
14. The Stone Warriors (Signet 1984)
15. Cheyenne Moon (Signet 1984)
16. High Vengeance (Signet 1984)
17. Drum Roll (Signet 1984)
18. Riverboat Queen (Signet 1985)
19. Frenchman's Pass (Signet 1985)
20. The Sonora Badman (Signet 1985)
21. The Denver Duchess (Signet 1985)
22. The Opium Queen (Signet 1985)
23. The Death Hunters (Signet 1985)
24. Flame River (Signet 1986)

163. KANE
By Lee Frank
Kane Richards trails the killers of his family, seeking revenge. The books are published in Warner and Paperback Library editions.
Kane (Warner 1971)
Kane and the Goldbar Killers (Warner 1973)
Kane and the Outlaw's Double Cross (Warner 1975)

164. MORGAN KANE, U.S. MARSHAL
By Louis Masterson
The series was translated from Norwegian for the British paperback series.
1. Without Mercy (Corgi)
2. The Claw of the Dragon (Corgi)
3. The Star and the Gun (Corgi)
4. Backed by the Law (Corgi)
5. A Ranger's Honour (Corgi)
6. Marshal and Murderer (Corgi)
7. Pistolero (Corgi)
8. The Monster from Yuma (Corgi)
9. The Devil's Marshal (Corgi)
10. Gunman's Inheritance (Corgi)
11. Revenge (Corgi)
12. Storm Over Sonora (Corgi)

13. The Law of the Jungle (Corgi)
14. No Tears for Morgan Kane (Corgi)
15. Between Life and Death (Corgi)
16. Return to Action (Corgi)
17. Rio Grande (Corgi)
18. Bravado (Corgi)
19. The Gallion Express (Corgi)
20. Ransom (Corgi)
21. Killing for the Law (Corgi)
22. The Butcher from Guerrero (Corgi)
23. Duel in Tombstone (Corgi)
24. To the Death, Senor Kane! (Corgi)
25. Hell Below Zero (Corgi)
26. Coyoteros! (Corgi)
27. Bloody Earth (Corgi)
28. New Orleans Gamble (Corgi)
29.
30. Apache Break-Out (Corgi 1975)

165. THE KANSAN
By Robert E. Mills
Davy Watson is the title character in this adult series.
1. Showdown at Hell's Canyon (Leisure 1980)
2. Across the High Sierras (Leisure 1980)
3. Red Apache Sun (Leisure 1981)
4. Judge Colt (Leisure 1981)
5. Warm Flesh and Hot Lead (Leisure 1981)
6. Long, Hard Ride (Leisure 1981)
7. Trail of Desire (Leisure 1981)
8. Shootout at the Golden Slipper (Leisure 1982)
9. The Kansan's Woman (Leisure 1982)
10. The Kansan's Lady (Leisure 1982)

166. THE KEN SERIES
By Basil Miller
This is a boys' book series published in paperback.
Ken Rides the Range (Zondervan)
Ken Bails Out (Zondervan)
Ken in Alaska (Zondervan)
Ken Saddles Up (Zondervan)
Ken on the Argentine Pampas (Zondervan)
Ken South of the Border (Zondervan)
Ken on the Navajo Trail (Zondervan)
Ken Follows the Chuck Wagon (Zondervan)
Ken Hits the Cowboy Trail (Zondervan)
Ken Range Detective (Zondervan)
Ken and the Cattle Thieves (Zondervan 1953)

167. DICK KENT SERIES
By Milton Richards
This boys' book series was also called Boys of the Royal Mounted Police
Series and the Northland Series.
Dick Kent with the Mounted Police (A.L. Burt 1927)
Dick Kent in the Far North (A.L Burt 1927)
Dick Kent with the Eskimos (A.L. Burt 1927)
Dick Kent, Fur Trader (A.L. Burt 1927)
Dick Kent with the Malamute Mail (A.L. Burt 1927)
Dick Kent on Special Duty (A.L. Burt 1928)
Dick Kent at Half Way House (A.L. Burt 1929)
Dick Kent, Mounted Police Deputy (A.L. Burt 1933)
Dick Kent's Mysterious Mission (A.L. Burt 1933)
Dick Kent and the Mine Mystery (A.L. Burt 1934)

168. LEE KERSHAW, MANHUNTER
By Gordon D. Sherriffs
Kershaw is a veteran manhunter and soldier of fortune.
Showdown in Sonora (Fawcett 1969)
The Manhunter (Fawcett 1970)
The Apache Hunter (Fawcett 1976)
The Marauders (Fawcett 1977)

169. QUINT KERSHAW
By Gordon D. Sherriffs
Kershaw is a mountain man in this adult saga series.
Now He Is Legend (Fawcett 1979)
The Untamed Breed (Fawcett 1981)
Bold Legend (Fawcett 1982)

170. KILBURN
By Sam Victor
Kilburn is a series written by Morris Herschman.
1. Kilburn (Berkley Medallion 1974)
2. Spikebit (Berkley Medallion 1974)
3. High Hazard (Berkley Medallion 1975)
4. Wolf Moon (Berkley Medallion 1975)
5. Rope Law (Berkley Medallion 1976)
6. Posse of Killers (Berkley Medallion 1976)

171. KIOGA, THE SNOW HAWK
By William L. Chester
These four books, originally serialized in *Blue Book* in 1935, '36, '37
and '38, are generally considered Lost Race novels and were reprinted
in paperback under a science fiction imprint. Still, the stories of a white
man, Lincoln Rand, shipwrecked and abandoned in Nato'wa, the nor-
thern ancestral homeland of the American Indians, and raised by
natives as Kioga, the Snow Hawk, have ties to the inhabitants of the

Western wilderness.
Hawk of the Wilderness (Harper 1936)
Kioga of the Wilderness (DAW 1976)
One Against a Wilderness (DAW 1977)
Kioga of the Unknown Land (DAW 1978)

172. DON KIRK SERIES
By Gilbert Patten
This is a boys' book series.
The Boy Cattle King or, Don Kirk (Street & Smith 1895)
The Boy from the West (Street & Smith 1894)
Don Kirk's Mine or, The Fight for a Lost Fortune (Street & Smith 1895)

173. KLAW
By W.L. Fieldhouse
John Klawson is missing his right hand. The series was later issued by
Leisure.
  1. Klaw (Tower 1980)
  2. Town of Blood (Tower 1981)
  3. The Rattler Gang (Tower 1981)

174. KUNG FU
By Howard Lee
The television series from 1972-75 featuring Kwai Chang Caine, martial
arts master, prompted this series.
  1. The Way of the Tiger, the Sign of the Dragon (Warner Paperback
Library)
  2. Chains (Warner Paperback Ligrary)
  3. Superstition (Warner Paperback Library)
  4. A Praying Mantis Kills (Warner Paperback Library 1974)

175. NEVADA JIM LACY
By Zane Grey and Romer Zane Grey
One of Zane Grey's best-selling titles, *Nevada* is about Jim Lacy, alias
Texas Jack, a cowboy wanted by both sides of the law. The book was
followed by novelettes in *Zane Grey's Western Magazine*, under the
Romer Zane Grey house name, which were collected.
Nevada (Harper 1928)
Nevada Jim Lacy: Beyond the Mogollon Rim (Tower 1980)

176. ADAM LAREY
By Zane Grey
Adam Larey is featured in the novel and sequel.
Wanderer of the Wasteland (Harper's 1923)
Stairs of Sand (Harper's 1943)

LARRY AND STREAK
See LARRY AND STETCH

177. LARRY AND STRETCH
By Marshall Grover
Larry Valentine and Stretch Emerson were featured in a long-running
Australian series of short paperback Westerns. For its American version,
Bantam changed the characters' names to Larry Vance and Streak
Everett and the author became Marshall McCoy. Belmont's brief reprint
series in the U.S. used the original character and author names. The
books were penned by Leonard F. Mears. Many of the books carry no
copyright date.
Drift (Scripts)
Colorado Pursuit (Scripts)
Born to Drift (Scripts)
Cold Trail to Kirby (Scripts)
Hell-Raisers (Scripts)
Rawhide River Ambush (Cleveland 1958)
Texans Are Trouble (Cleveland 1958)
Half-Cold Trail (Cleveland 1959)
Ride Out, Texans (Cleveland 1959)
Seventeen Guns (Cleveland 1959)
Texas Drifters (Cleveland 1959)
Ride Reckless (Scripts)
Greenback Fever (Scripts)
Fast, Free and Texan (Scripts)
The Feuders (Scripts)
The Four O'Clock Fracas (Scripts)
Here Lies Andy McGraw (Scripts)
Seven for Banner Pass (Scripts)
Doom Trail (Scripts)
First Kill (Scripts)
Devil's Dinero (Scripts)
Lone Star Valiant (Horwitz)
Lone Star Hellions (Horwitz)
Lone Star Reckoning (Horwitz)
Lone Star Fury (Horwitz)
Lone Star Reckless (Horwitz)
Lone Star Vengeance (Horwitz)
Lone Star Firebrands (Horwitz)
Lone Star Bodyguards (Horwitz)
Lone Star Lucky (Horwitz)
The Emerson Challenge (Horwitz)
Texans Die Hard (Horwitz)
Texans Never Quit (Horwitz)
Tall, Tough, and Texan (Horwitz)
Trail Dust (Horwitz)
Start Shooting, Texans (Horwitz)
Texans Walk Proud (Horwitz)
Texas Ghost Gun (Horwitz)
Tall Riders (Horwitz)

North of Texas (Horwitz)
We're From Texas (Horwitz)
The Wayward Kind (Horwitz)
Wild Trail to Denver (Horwitz)
Noon Train to Breslow (Horwitz)
The Eyes of Texas (Horwitz)
Decoys from Hell (Horwitz)
Day of the Posse (Horwitz)
Now... Texans (Horwitz)
Texan in My Sights (Horwitz)
Saludos, Texans (Horwitz)
Back in Texas (Horwitz)
Defiant Texans (Horwitz)
Bend of the River (Horwitz)
Bravados from Texas (Horwitz)
Close In for a Showdown (Horwitz)
Follow the Texans (Horwitz)
Rogue Calibre (Horowitz)
Too Many Texans (Horowitz)
Find Kell Wade (Horowitz)
Ride Slow, Ride Wary (Horwitz)
Nobody Wants Reilly (Horwitz)
This Range is Mine (Horwitz)
Rob a Bank in Kansas (Horwitz)
Arizona Wild-Cat (Horwitz)
Ride Out Shooting (Horwitz)
Ride Wild to Glory (Horwitz)
Border Storm (Horwitz)
Draw, Aim, and Fire (Horwitz)
Never Prod a Texan (Horwitz)
The Fast Right Hand (Horwitz)
Don't Count the Odds (Horwitz)
Face the Gun (Horwitz)
Decoys from Texas (Horwitz)
A Bullet is Faster (Horwitz)
Gun Glory for Texans (Scripts 1967) (Bantam)
Lone Star Rowdy (Scripts 1967)
Many a Wild Mile (Scripts 1967)
Trouble Trail Yonder (Scripts 1967) (Bantam)
Two Tall Strangers (Scripts 1967)
Boom Town Bravados (Scripts 1967)
Legend of Bell Canyon (Scripts 1967) (Bantam 1968)
The Texans Came Shooting (Scripts 1967)
Tombstone for a Fugitive (Scripts 1967)
Too Tough for San Remo (Scripts 1968) (Bantam)
Amarillo Ridge (Horowitz 1968)
The Bar G Bunch (Horowitz 1968)
High Spade (Horowitz 1968)

Kin to the Wild Wind (Horwitz 1968)
Wyoming Thunder (Horwitz 1968)
Big Day at Blue Creek (Horwitz 1968) (Bantam 1968)
Wheels Out of Jericho (Horwitz 1968) (Bantam 1968)
Calaboose Canyon (Horwitz 1969)
The Garrard Heritage (Horwitz 1969)
The Glory Wagon (Horwitz 1969)
Hot Sky Over Paraiso (Horwitz 1969)
Hour of Jeopardy (Horwitz 1969)
Turn and Fire (Cleveland 1969)
Three Trails to Modoc (Horwitz 1969) (Bantam 1969)
Two for the Gallows (Horwitz 1969)
Feud at Mendoza (Belmont 1969)
Trouble is Our Shadow (Cleveland 1970)
All the Tall Men (Cleveland 1970)
The Big Dinero (Cleveland 1970)
Crisis in Babylon (Cleveland 1970)
The Freebooters (Cleveland 1970)
Gun Fury at Sun-Up (Horwitz 1970)
Guns Across the Rockies (Horwitz 1970)
Gunsmoke Challenge (Cleveland 1970)
Our Kind of Law (Horwitz 1970)
Saturday Night in Candle Rock (Horwitz 1970)
Texas Rampage (Cleveland 1970)
Born to Ramble (Horwitz 1970)
The Noose-Cheaters (Horwitz 1970)
They Won't Forget Sweeney (Horitz 1971)
7 for Banner Pass (Horwitz 1971)
Montana Runaway (Horwitz 1972)
The Hellion Breed (Horwitz 1972)
Rampage at Rico Bend (Horwitz 1972)
Gunsmoke in Utopia (Horwitz 1973)
Hangrope for Beaumont (Horwitz 1973)
The Last Ambush (Horwitz 1973)
McCracken's Marauders (Horwitz 1973)
Mexican Jackpot (Horwitz 1973)
War Dance at Red Canyon (Horwitz 1973)
Cold-Eye Cordell (Horwitz 1973)
The Desperate Hours (Horwitz 1973)
Guns for the Ladies (Horwitz 1973)
Madigan's Day (Horwitz 1973)
Red Bandana (Horwitz 1973)
Who Killed Rice? (Horwitz 1973)
Dakota Red (Horwitz 1974)
Get Goin', Greeley! (Horwitz 1974)
High Country Shootout (Horwitz 1974)
The Odds Against O'Shea (Horwitz 1974)
Doom Trail (Horwitz 1974)

Hijacker's Noon (Horwitz 1974)
Man on Pulpit Rock (Horwitz 1974)
The Predators (Horwitz 1974)
Saddletramp Justice (Horwitz 1974)
Tin Stars for Tall Texans (Horwitz 1974)
Damn Outlaws (Horwitz 1975)
They'll Hang Billy for Sure (Horwitz 1974)
Too Many Enemies (Horwitz 1974)
Delaney and the Drifters (Horwitz 1975)
Dollar Trail to Ramirez (Horwitz 1975)
The Last Challenge (Horwitz 1975)
Rescue Party (Horwitz 1975)
Winners and Losers (Horwitz 1975)
The Battle of Blunder Ridge (Horwitz 1976)
The Calaboose Gang (Horwitz 1976)
Colorado Belle (Horwitz 1976)
Kiss the Loot Goodbye (Horwitz 1976)
Outcasts of Sabado Creek (Horwitz 1976)
Dawson Died Twice (Horwitz 1976)
Follow That Train (Horwitz 1976)
Twenty Seven Rifles (Horwitz 1976)
The Bandit Trap (Horwitz 1976)
Before He Kills Again (Horwitz 1976)
Guns of the Valiant (Horwitz 1976)
Prelude to a Showdown (Horwitz 1976)
Raid a Painted Wagon (Horwitz 1976)
Suddenly a Hero (Horwitz 1976)
The Sundown Seven (Horwitz 1976)
Track of the Lawless (Horwitz 1976)
3 Days in Davisburg (Horwitz 1977)
8.10 from Verdugo (Horwitz 1977)
After the Payoff (Horwitz 1977)
Bullion Route (Horwitz 1977)
California Runaround (Horwitz 1977)
Dealer Takes Three (Horwitz 1977)
Everything Happens to Holley (Horwitz 1977)
Jokers Wild (Horwitz 1977)
Kansas Hex (Horwitz 1977)
Left Hand Luke (Horwitz 1977)
Lone Star Godfathers (Horwitz 1977)
Midnight Marauders (Horwitz 1977)
The Only Bank in Town (Horwitz 1977)
Royal Target (Horwitz 1977)
Beecher's Quest (Horwitz 1977)
Eight Defiant Men (Horwitz 1977)
Ghost of a Chance (Horwitz 1977)
Trouble Shooters Die Hard (Horwitz 1977)
Bullet for a Widow (Horwitz 1978)

Calaboose Express (Horwitz 1978)
Dinero Fever (Horwitz 1978)
Double Shuffle (Horwitz 1978)
Fogarty's War (Horwitz 1978)
Gold, Guns, and the Girl (Horwitz 1978)
Hammer's Horde (Horwitz 1978)
In Memory of Marty Malone (Horwitz 1978)
Mark of the Star (Horwitz 1978)
Nebraska Trackdown (Horwitz 1978)
The Rescuers Ride West (Horwitz 1978)
Last Stage to Delarno (Horwitz 1978)
Wyoming Long Shot (Horwitz 1978)
Baker Street Breakout (Horwitz 1979)
Both Sides of Battle Creek (Horwitz 1979)
Dead Man's Share (Horwitz 1979)
The Doomed of Mesa Rico (Horwitz 1979)
Fort Dillon (Horwitz 1979)
High Stakeout (Horwitz 1979)
Keep Allison Alive (Horwitz 1979)
Pearson County Raiders (Horwitz 1979)
Run from the Buzzards (Horwitz 1979)
Phantom of Fortuna (Horwitz 1979)
Turn the Key on Emerson (Horwitz 1979)
The Women from Whitlock (Horwitz 1979)
Brady's Back in Town (Horwitz 1979)
In Pursuit of Quincey Budd (Horwits 1979)
Posse Plus Two (Horwitz 1979)
The Seventh Guilty Man (Horwitz 1979)
They Came to Jurado (Horwitz 1979)
4 Aces and the Knave (Horwitz 1980)
El Capitan's Enemies (Horwitz 1980)
Day of the Killers (Horwitz 1980)
Death Quest (Horwitz 1980)
Going Straight in Frisbee (Horwitz 1980)
Hackett's Gold (Horwitz 1980)
One More Showdown (Horwitz 1980)
Prey of the Rogue Riders (Horwitz 1980)
Ride Boldly in Dakota (Horwitz 1980)
Rough Night for the Guilty (Horwitz 1980)
Siege of Jericho (Horwitz 1980)
Vengeance in Spades (Horwitz 1980)
Wait for the Judge (Horwitz 1980)
Wrong Name on a Tombstone (Horwitz 1980)
Doc Rance of Rambeau (Horwitz 1980)
Gun Reckoning at Gruncy's Grave (Horwitz 1980)
He's Valentine, I'm Emerson (Horwitz 1980)
Kid Light Fingers (Horwitz 1980)
Lady is a Target (Horwitz 1980)
Twenty Year Man (Horwitz 1980)

178. LASHTROW
By Roe Richmond
Ranger Lash Lashtrow's adventures have been published by two companies.
1. Crusade on the Chisholm (Leisure 1980)
2. Rio Grande Riptide (Leisure 1980)
3. Hell on a Holiday (Leisure 1980)
4. Guns at Goliad (Leisure 1980)
5. Nevada Queen High (Leisure 1980)
6. Lifeline of Texas (Leisure 1981)
7. Staked Plains Rendezvous (Leisure 1981)
El Paso Del Norte (Ace Charter 1982)

179. LASSITER (I)
By Zane Grey and Loren Zane Grey
Zane Grey's gunman Lassiter has been revived for a new series using his son Loren Zane Grey's name as a house name. *Riders* was originally serialized in *Field & Stream, Rainbow* in *Argosy.*
Riders of the Purple Sage by Zane Grey (Harper 1912)
The Rainbow Trail by Zane Grey (Harper 1915)
1. Lassiter by Loren Zane Grey (Pocket 1985)
2. Ambush for Lassiter by Loren Zane Grey (Pocket 1985)
3. Lassiter's Gold by Loren Zane Grey (Pocket 1986)

180 LASSITER (II)
By Jack Slade
Lassiter is a hard-nosed cowboy in this long-running series which has appeared under Belmont Tower, Tower and Unibook imprints. Willis Todhunter Ballard wrote some of the entries.
Lassiter (by Willis Todhunter Ballard) (Belmont Tower 1968)
The Man from Yuma (by Ballard) (Belmont Tower 1968)
The Man from Cheyenne (by Ballard) (Belmont Tower 1968)
Sidewinder (Belmont Tower 1968)
The Man from Del Rio (Belmont Tower 1969)
A Hell of a Way to Die (Belmont Tower 1971)
Guerilla (Belmont Tower 1972)
The Man from Lordsburg (Belmont Tower 1973)
Gunfight at Ringo Junction (Belmont Tower 1973)
Gutshot (Belmont Tower 1973)
High Lonesome (Belmont Tower 1973)
The Badlanders (Belmont Tower 1973)
Hell at Yuma (Belmont Tower 1974)
The Man from Tombstone (Belmont Tower 1974)
Rimfire (Belmont Tower 1974)
Ride into Hell (Belmont Tower 1974)
Blood River (Belmont Tower 1974)
Durango Bill (Belmont Tower 1975)
Apache Junction (Belmont Tower 1975)

The Man from Papago Wells (Belmont Tower 1976)
Cattle Baron (Belmont Tower 1977)
Hangman (Belmont Tower 1977)
Lust for Gold (Belmont Tower 1977)
Wolverine (Belmont Tower 1978)
Five Graves for Lassiter (Belmont Tower 1979)
Canyon Kill (Tower 1979)
Blood Knife (Tower 1979)
Big Foot's Range (Belmont Tower 1979)
Redgate Gold (Tower 1981)
Funeral Bend (Belmont Tower)
Brother Gun (Tower)

181. LATIGO
By Dean Owen
Latigo seeks vengeance after he finds his family murdered by a ruthless
railroad tycoon and his hired guns. The series is based on the Field
Enterprises comic strip by Stan Lynde, who also wrote and drew the
Rick O'Shay Western comic strip (*Rick O'Shay and Hipshot*, Tempo
1976).
  1. Trackdown (Popular Library 1981)
  2. Vengeance Trail (Popular Library 1981)
  3. Dead Shot (Popular Library 1981)
  4. Double Eagle (Popular Library 1982)

182. LAWMAN (I)
By J.B. Dancer
John B. Harvey is one of the writers of this series.
  1. Evil Breed (Coronet 1977)
  2.
  3. Judgement Day (Coronet 1978)
  4
  5. The Hanged Man (Coronet 1979)

183. LAWMAN (II)
By Mike Newton
U.S. Marshal Joshua Creed is the Lawman.
  1. Creed's Vengeance (Carousel Westerns)
  2. Creed's Gold (Carousel Westerns)
  3. Creed's War (Carousel Westerns)
  4. Creed's Kill (Carousel Westerns)
  5. Creed's Treasure (Carousel Westerns)
  6. Creed's Hell (Carousel Westerns 1982)
  7. Creed's Vendetta (Carousel Westerns 1982)
  8. Creed's Ransom (Carousel Westerns)
  9. Creed's Gauntlet (Carousel Westerns 1982)

184. LT. JOE LEAPHORN
By Tony Hillerman
The leading character is a contemporary Indian police officer. The books were reprinted in paper by Avon.
The Blessing Way (Harper 1970) (Macmillan 1970)
Dance Hall of the Dead (Harper 1973)
Listening Woman (Harper 1978) (Macmillan 1979)

185. LEATHER AND LACE
By Various Authors
This is an adult series aimed at women readers.
1. The Lavender Blossom by Dorothy Dixon (Zebra 1982)
2. The Trembling Heart by Dixon (Zebra 1982)
3. The Belle of the Rio Grande by Dixon (Zebra 1982)
4. Flame of the West by Dixon (Zebra 1982)
5. Cimarron Rose by Dixon (Zebra 1982)
6. Honesuckle Love by Carolyn T. Armstrong (Zebra 1983)
7. Diamond Queen by Dixon (Zebra 1983)
8. Texas Wildflower by Tammie Lee (Zebra 1983)
9. Yellowstone Jewel by Dixon (Zebra 1985)

186. LEATHERHAND
By Mike Wales
Vent Torrey, Leatherhand, is an expert gun despite an injury which left his gunhand little more than a leather contraption.
1. Leatherhand (Pinnacle 1983)
2. Hangman's Legacy (Pinnacle 1983)
3. Lottery of Death (Pinnacle 1984)
4. Dead Wrong (Pinnacle 1984)
5. Bad Day at Bandera (Pinnacle 1984)
6. The Magician (Pinnacle 1985)
7. The Last Ride (Pinnacle 1985)
8. Dark Nemesis (Pinnacle 1985)

187. LITTLE HOUSE ON THE PRAIRIE
By Laura Wilder Ingalls
The story of the Ingalls family in the northwest later became a television series (1974-83).
Little House in the Big Woods (Harper 1932)
Little House on the Prairie (Harper 1935)
On the Banks of Plow Creek (Harper 1937)
By the Shores of Silver Lake (Harper 1939)
Long Winter (Harper 1940)
Little Town on the Prairie (Harper 1941)
These Happy Golden Years (Harper 1943)
The First Four Years (Harper 1971)

188. LOBO
By Dennis Crafton

Galen LeBeau is a gunslinger in this adult series.
1. Silver Showdown (Pinnacle 1982)
2. Commanche Duel (Pinnacle 1982)

189. JOHNNY LOGAN
By D.B. Newton
Logan is a Cheyenne raised by whites. The author is Dwight Bennett Newton.
Massacre Valley (Curtis 1973)
Trail of the Bear (Popular Library 1975)
The Land Grabbers (Popular Library 1975)

190. JABE LOMAX, BORDER PEACE OFFICER
By G.J. Morgan
The writer is actually Donald S. Rowland. The series is about a former Confederate army man now a peace officer in Texas. The book is listed as the first in a series.
Border Fury (Futura 1975)

191. THE LONE RANGER
By Fran Striker and Gary McCarthy
The famous masked man of radio (1933-55), television drama (1949-57) with Clayton Moore and Jay Silverheels), television cartoon (1966-69) and motion pictures (three features and one serial) appeared in a series of boys' books with his Indian companion Tonto in the 1930s, '40s and '50s. Seven of the books were reprinted in paperback by Pinnacle, in an-in anticipation of the 1981 movie. Six of the Grosset & Dunlap books were rewrites of novels originally published in *The Lone Ranger Magazine* in 1937.
The Lone Ranger by Fran Striker (by Gaylord DuBois in first edition) (Grosset & Dunlap 1936)
The Lone Ranger and the Gold Robbery by Striker (Grosset & Dunlap 1939)
The Lone Ranger and the Mystery Ranch by Striker (Grosset & Dunlap 1938)
The Lone Ranger and the Outlaw Stronghold by Striker (Grosset & Dunlap 1939)
The Lone Ranger and Tonto by Striker (Grosset & Dunlap 1940)
The Lone Ranger and the Haunted Gulch by Striker (Grosset & Dunlap 1941)
The Lone Ranger Rides by Striker (Putnam's 1941)
The Lone Ranger Traps the Smugglers by Striker (Grosset & Dunlap 1942)
The Lone Ranger Rides Again by Striker (Grosset & Dunlap 1943)
The Lone Ranger Rides North by Striker (Grosset & Dunlap 1946)
The Lone Ranger and the Silver Bullet by Striker (Grosset & Dunlap 1947)
The Lone Ranger on Powderhorn Trail by Striker (Grosset & Dunlap 1949)

The Lone Ranger in Wild Horse Canyon by Striker (Grosset & Dunlap 1950)
The Lone Ranger West of Maverick Pass by Striker (Grosset & Dunlap 1951)
The Lone Ranger's New Deputy by Striker (Simon and Shuster 1951)
The Lone Ranger at Gunsight Mesa by Striker (Grosset & Dunlap 1953)
The Lone Ranger and the Bitter Spring Feud by Striker (Grosset & Dunlap 1954)
The Lone Ranger and Trouble on the Santa Fe by Striker (Grosset & Dunlap 1955)
The Lone Ranger on the Red Butte Trail by Striker (Grosset & Dunlap 1956)
The Lone Ranger and the Code of the West by Striker (Grosset & Dunlap 1957)
The Legend of the Lone Ranger by Gary McCarthy (Ballantine 1981)

192. LONE STAR
By Wesley Ellis
Jessica Starbuck shoots like a man, loves like a woman. Her companion is Ki, a martial arts expert who rides with her to protect the Starbuck empire, in this adult series. The author is presumably a pseudonym. See also Longarm and Lone Star series entry.
1. Lone Star on the Treachery Trail (Jove 1982)
2. Lone Star and the Opium Rustlers (Jove 1982)
3. Lone Star and the Border Bandits (Jove 1982)
4. Lone Star and the Kansas Wolves (Jove 1982)
5. Lone Star and the Utah Kid (Jove 1982)
6. Lone Star and the Land Grabbers (Jove 1982)
7. Lone Star in the Tall Timber (Jove 1983)
8. Lone Star and the Showdowners (Jove 1983)
9. Lone Star and the Hardrock Payoff (Jove 1983)
10. Lone Star and the Renegade Comanches (Jove 1983)
11. Lone Star on Outlaw Mountain (Jove 1983)
12. Lone Star and the Gold Raiders (Jove 1983)
13. Lone Star and the Denver Madam (Jove 1983)
14. Lone Star and the Railroad War (Jove 1983)
15. Lone Star and the Mexican Standoff (Jove 1983)
16. Lone Star and the Badlands War (Jove 1983)
17. Lone Star and the San Antonio Rais (Jove 1983)
18. Lone Star and the Ghost Pirates (Jove 1984)
19. Lone Star and the Owlhoot Trail (Jove 1984)
20. Lone Star and the Devil's Trail (Jove 1984)
21. Lone Star and the Apache Revenge (Jove 1984)
22. Lone Star and the Texas Gambler (Jove 1984)
23. Lone Star and the Hangrope Heritage (Jove 1984)
24. Lone Star and the Montana Troubles (Jove 1984)
25. Lone Star and the Mountain Man (Jove 1984)
26. Lone Star and the Stockyard Showdown (Jove 1984)
27. Lone Star and the Riverboat Gamblers (Jove 1984)

28. Lone Star and the Mescalero Outlaws (Jove 1984)
29. Lone Star and the Amarillo Rifles (Jove 1985)
30. Lone Star and the School for Outlaws (Jove 1985)
31. Lone Star on the Treasure River (Jove 1985)
32. Lone Star and the Moon Trail Feud (Jove 1985)
33. Lone Star and the Golden Mesa (Jove 1985)
34. Lone Star and the Rio Grande Bandits (Jove 1985)
35. Lone Star and the Buffalo Hunters (Jove 1985)
36. Lone Star and the Biggest Gun in the West (Jove 1985)
37. Lone Star and the Apache Warrior (Jove 1985)
38. Lone Star and the Gold Mine War (Jove 1985)
39. Lone Star and the California Oil War (Jove 1985)
40. Lone Star and the Alaskan Guns (Jove 1985)
41. Lone Star and the White River Curse (Jove 1986)
42. Lone Star and the Tombstone Gamble (Jove 1986)
43. Lone Star and the Timberland Terror (Jove 1986)
44. Lone Star in the Cherokee Strip (Jove 1986)
45. Lone Star and the Oregon Trail (Jove 1986)

193. THE LONER
By Robert L. Trimnell
Harry Keel's military career came to an end when he refused to kill helpless Indians. From then on, he was a Loner.
1. Colorado Kill (Manor 1974)
2. New Mexico Massacre (Manor)
3. Winslow Freight (Manor 1975)
4. Hell on Legg's Hill (Manor 1976)

194. LONGARM
By Tabor Evans
Custis Long, Longarm, is a ranger in the employ of Billy Vail, Chief United States Marshal for the·First District of Colorado, in this adult series. Several writers are masked by the house name, including Lou Cameron, Will C. Knott, Harry Whittington and Mel Marshall. See also next entry.
1. Longarm (Jove 1978)
2. Longarm on the Border (Jove 1978)
3. Longarm and the Avenging Angels (Jove 1978)
4. Longarm and the Windigo (Jove 1978)
5. Longarm in the Indian Nations (Jove 1979)
6. Longarm and the Loggers (Jove 1979)
7. Longarm and the Highgraders (Jove 1979)
8. Longarm and the Nesters (Jove 1979)
9. Longarm and the Hatchet Men (Jove 1979)
10. Longarm and the Molly Maguires (Jove 1979)
11. Longarm and the Texas Rangers (Jove 1979)
12. Longarm in Lincoln County (Jove 1979)
13. Longarm in the Sand Hills (Jove 1979)

14. Longarm in Leadville (Jove 1979)
15. Longarm on the Devil's Trail (Jove 1979)
16. Longarm and the Mounties (Jove 1979)
17. Longarm and the Bandit Queen (Jove 1980)
18. Longarm on the Yellowstone (Jove 1980)
19. Longarm in the Four Corners (Jove 1980)
20. Longarm at Robber's Roost (Jove 1980)
21. Longarm and the Sheep Herders (Jove 1980)
22. Longarm and the Ghost Dancers (Jove 1980)
23. Longarm and the Town Tamer (Jove 1980)
24. Longarm and the Railroaders (Jove 1980)
25. Longarm on the Old Mission Trail (Jove 1980)
26. Longarm and the Dragon Hunters (Jove 1980)
27. Longarm and the Rurales (Jove 1980)
28. Longarm on the Humbolt (by Harry Whittington) (Jove 1981)
29. Longarm on the Big Muddy (Jove 1981)
30. Longarm South of the Gila (Jove 1981)
31. Longarm in Northfield (Jove 1981)
32. Longarm and the Golden Lady (by Whittington) (Jove 1981)
33. Longarm and the Laredo Loop (Jove 1981)
34. Longarm and the Boot Hillers (Jove 1981)
35. Longarm and the Blue Norther (by Whittington) (Jove 1981)
36. Longarm on the Santa Fe (Jove 1981)
37. Longarm and the Stalking Corpse (Jove 1981)
38. Longarm and the Comancheros (Jove 1981)
39. Longarm and the Devil's Railroad (Jove 1981)
40. Longarm in Silver City (by Whittington) (Jove 1982)
41. Longarm on the Barbary Coast (Jove 1982)
42. Longarm and the Moonshiners (Jove 1982)
43. Longarm in Yuma (Jove 1982)
44. Longarm in Boulder Canyon (by Whittington) (Jove 1982)
45. Longarm in Deadwood (Jove 1982)
46. Longarm and the Great Train Robbery (Jove 1982)
47. Longarm in the Badlands (Jove 1982)
48. Longarm in the Big Thicket (by Whittington) (Jove 1982)
49. Longarm and the Eastern Dudes (Jove 1982)
50. Longarm in the Big Bend (Jove 1982)
51. Longarm and the Snake Dancers (Jove 1983)
52. Longarm and the Great Divide (Jove 1983)
53. Longarm and the Buckskin Rogue (Jove 1983)
54. Longarm and the Calico Kid (Jove 1983)
55. Longarm and the French Actress (Jove 1983)
56. Longarm and the Outlaw Gunmen (Jove 1983)
57. Longarm and the Bounty Hunters (Jove 1983)
58. Longarm in No Man's Land (Jove 1983)
59. Longarm and the Big Outfit (Jove 1983)
60. Longarm and Santa Anna's Gold (Jove 1983)
61. Longarm and the Custer County War (Jove 1983)

62. Longarm in Virginia City (Jove 1983)
63. Longarm and the James County War (Jove 1983)
64. Longarm and the Cattle Baron (Jove 1983)
65. Longarm and the Steer Swindlers (Jove 1984)
66. Longarm and the Hangman's Noose (Jove 1984)
67. Longarm and the Omaha Tinhorns (Jove 1984)
68. Longarm and the Desert Duchess (Jove 1984)
69. Longarm of the Painted Desert (Jove 1984)
70. Longarm on the Oglalla Trail (Jove 1984)
71. Longarm on the Arkansas (Jove 1984)
72. Longarm and the Blindman's Vengeance (1984)
73. Longarm at Fort Reno (Jove 1985)
74. Longarm and the Durango Payroll (Jove 1985)
75. Longarm West of the Pecos (Jove 1985)
76. Longarm on the Nevada Line (Jove 1985)
77. Longarm and the Blackfoot Guns (Jove 1985)
78. Longarm on the Santa Cruz (Jove 1985)
79. Longarm and the Cowboy's Revenge (Jove 1985)
80. Longarm on the Goodnight Trail (Jove 1985)
81. Longarm and the Frontier Duchess (Jove 1985)
82. Longarm in the Bitteroots (Jove 1985)
83. Longarm and the Tenderfoot (Jove 1985)
84. Longarm and the Stagecoach Bandits (Jove 1985)
85. Longarm and the Big Shootout (Jove 1986)
86. Longarm in the Hardrock Country (Jove 1986)
87. Longarm in the Texas Panhandle (Jove 1986)
88. Longarm and the Rancher's Showdown (Jove 1986)
89. Longarm and the Inland Passage (Jove 1986)

195. LONGARM AND LONE STAR
By Tabor Evans
This annual series features two of the publisher's series heroes.
Longarm and the Lone Star Legend (Jove 1982)
Longarm and the Lone Star Vengeance (Jove 1983)
Longarm and the Lone Star Bounty (Jove 1984)
Longarm and the Lone Star Rescue (Jove 1985)
Longarm and the Lone Star Deliverance (Jove 1986)

196. LONG TRAIL SERIES
By Dale Wilkins
Josephine Chase penned this boys' book series.
The Long Trail Boys at Sweet Water Ranch or, The Mystery of the White Shadow (John C. Winston 1923)
The Long Trail Boys and the Gray Cloaks or, The Mystery of the Night Riders (John C. Winston 1923)
The Long Trail Boys and the Scarlet Sign (John C. Winston 1925)
The Long Trail Boys and the Vanishing Rider (John C. Winston 1925)
The Long Trail Boys and the Mystery of the Fingerprints (John C.

Winston 1928)
The Long Trail Boys and the Mystery of the Unknown Messenger
(John C. Winston 1928)

197. SHERIFF MOSS MAGILL
By Dorothy Gardiner
There is a lot of historical detail in this writer's works.
What Crime Is It? (Doubleday 1949) The Case of the Hula Clock (Hammond 1957)
The Seventh Mourner (Doubleday 1958)
Lion in Wait (Doubleday 1963) Lion? or Murder? (Hammond 1964)

198. THE MAKING OF AMERICA
By Various Authors
This saga series investigates a different aspect of early American history
in each volume; not all pertain to the West. The first 10 or so books appeared under the authors' real names, then all appeared under the Lee
Davis Willoughby house name. Real authors' names are given based on
copyright notices. The books appear under the James A. Bryans imprint.
1. The Wilderness Seekers by Lou Cameron (Dell)
2. The Mountain Breed by Aaron Fletcher (Dell)
3. The Conestoga People by Jeanne Sommers (Dell 1979)
4. The Forty-Niners by John Toombs (Dell)
5. Hearts Divided by Paula Moore (Dell)
6. The Builders by Sommers (Dell)
7. The Land Rushers by Elizabeth Zachery (Dell)
8. The Wild and the Wayward by Georgia Granger (Dell)
9. The Texans by John Toombs (Dell)
10. The Alaskans by Barry Myers (Dell)
11. The Golden Staters by Lee Davis Willoughby (Dell 1980)
12. The River People by Willoughby (by Greg Hunt) (Dell 1981)
13. The Landgrabbers by Willoughby (by Myers) (Dell 1981)
14. The Ranchers by Willoughby (by Robert Vaughan) (Del 1981)
15. The Homesteaders by Willoughby (Dell 1981)
16. The Frontier Healers by Willoughby (by Fletcher) (Dell 1981)
17. The Buffalo People by Willoughby (by Myers) (Dell 1981)
18. The Border Breed by Willoughby (by Toombs) (Dell 1981)
19. The Far Islanders by Willoughby (by Vaughan) (Dell 1981)
20. The Boomers by Willoughby (by Charles Beardsley) (Dell)
21. The Wildcatters by Willoughby (Dell)
22. The Gunfighters by Willoughby (by Michael Avallone) (Dell)
23. The Cajuns by Willoughby (by Jean Francis Webb) (Dell)
24. The Donner People by Willoughby (by Myers) (Dell 1982)
25. The Creoles by Willoughby (by Toombs) (Dell 1982)
26. The Nightriders by Willoughby (Dell 1982)
27. The Sooners by Willoughby (Dell 1982)
28. The Express Riders by Willoughby (Dell 1982)
29. The Vigilantes by Willoughby (by Ward Davis) (Dell 1982)

30. The Soldiers of Fortune by Willoughby (by George Ryan) (Dell 1982)
31. The Wranglers by Willoughby (by Karl Myer) (Dell 1982)
32. The Baja People by Willoughby (Dell 1983)
33. The Yukon Breed by Willoughby (by Myers) (Dell 1983)
34. The Smugglers by Willoughby (Dell 1983)
35. The Voyageurs by Willoughby (by William L. DeAndrea) (Dell 1983)
36. The Barbary Coasters by Willoughby (Dell 1983)
37. The Whalers by Willoughby (Dell 1983)
38. The Canadians by Willoughby (by Tad Richards) (Dell 1983)
39. The Prophet's People by Willoughby (by Leo P. Kelley) (Dell 1983)
40. The Lawmen by Willoughby (by Richard Laymon) (Dell 1983)
41. The Copper Kings by Willoughby (by Cameron) (Dell 1983)
42. The Caribbeans by Willoughby (by Walter Wager) (Dell 1983)
43. The Trail Blazers by Willoughby (Dell 1983)
44. The Gamblers by Willoughby (by Ian McMahan) (Dell 1983)
45. The Robber Barons by Willoughby (Dell 1983)
46. The Assassins by Willoughby (by James Seafidel) (Dell 1984)
47. The Bounty Hunters by Willoughy (Dell 1984)
48. The Texas Rangers by Willougby (Dell 1984)
49. The Outlaws by Willoughby (Dell 1984)
50. The Fugitives by Willoughby (Dell 1984)
51. The Frontier Detectives by Willoughby (Dell 1984)
52. The Raiders by Willoughby (Dell 1984)
53. The Rough Riders by Willoughby (Dell 1984)
54. Warriors of the Code by Willoughby (by Vaughan) (Dell 1985)
55. The Scarlet Sisters by Willoughby (by Myers) (Dell 1985)
56. The Sixgun Apostles by Willoughby (by Avallone) (Dell 1985)

MAKING OF AMERICA PART 2
See WOMEN WHO WON THE WEST

199. TWISTER MALONE
By Davis Dresser
The books feature Malone and his sidekick Chuckaluck Thompson.
    Death Rides the Pecos (Morrow 1940) (Ward Lock 1940)
    The Hangmen of Sleepy Valley (Morrow 1940) The Masked Riders of Sleepy Valley (Ward Lock 1941)
    Lynch-Rope Law (Morrow 1941) (Ward Lock 1942)
    Murder on the Mesa (Ward Lock 1953)

200. THE MAN WITH NO NAME
By Various Authors
This series is based on the Sergio Leone films starring Clint Eastwood. The novelisation of the first movie, printed in England, was not included in the American series. Award put out two editions of the books and Charter later issued at least two of the titles.

A Fistful of Dollars by Frank Chandler (by Terry Harknett) (Tandem 1972)
  For A Few Dollars More by Joe Millard (Award 1965) (Star 1980)
  The Good, The Bad, The Ugly by Millard (Award 1967) (Tandem 1968)
  A Dollar To Die For by Brian Fox (W.T. Ballard) (Award 1968)
  A Coffin Full Of Dollars by Millard (Award 1971) (Tandem 1972)
  The Million-Dollar Bloodhunt by Millard (Award 1973) (Tandem 1974)
  The Devil's Dollar Sign by Millard (Award 1973) (Tandem 1973)
  Blood for a Dirty Dollar by Millard (Award 1973) (Tandem 1974)

201. THE MASKED RIDER
By Various Authors
Rather than masking several hands behind a house name, as was common with most publishers, this series' writers were clearly bylined. The Masked Rider was featured in his own pulp magazine, *Masked Rider Western*, which began in 1934. The books are reprints of these stories. The Lone Ranger look-alike was Wayne Morgan, who roamed the West delivering justice with his faithful Indian companion Blue Hawk.
  Six-Gun Empire by Donald Bayne Hobart (Curtis 1965)
  Iron-Horse Gunsmoke by Hobart (Curtis 1965)
  Warrior Range by Hobart (Curtis 1966)
  Guns of the Big Hills by Hobart (Curtis 1966)
  Gallows Gold by Hobart (Curtis 1966)
  Vulture Valley by Hobart (Curtis 1967)
  Ambush at Big Creek Bridge by Hobart (Curtis 1967)
  Black Stallion Mesa by Hobart (Curtis 1967)
  Haunted Mesa by Hobart (Curtis 1967)
  Gunsmoke Country by Hobart (Curtis 1967)
  Red River Guns by Hobart (Curtis 1967)
  The Longhorn Trail by Hobart (Curtis 1967)
  Guns of the Clan by William L. Hopson (Curtis 1967)
  Desert of Doom by Hobart (Curtis)
  Guns Along the River by Hobart (Curtis 1968)
  Sinister Ranch (Curtis 1968)
  Warrior Range by Hobart (Curtis 1968)
  Desolation Range by Hobart (Curtis)
  The Lobo Trail by Larry Harris (Curtis)
  Chaparral Marauders by Tom Curry (Curtis)
  Two Rails West by Walker A. Tompkins (Curtis 1969)
  Ghost Mine Gold by Tompkins (Curtis 1969)
  Boom Town Guns by Hopson (Curtis)
  Gun Trail to Spanish Gold by C. William Harrison (Curtis 1970)
  Owlhoot Justice by Eugene A. Clancy (Curtis)

202. JIM MASON
By Elmer Russell Gregor
This is a boys' book series.
  Jim Mason, Backwoodsman (D. Appleton 1923)

Jim Mason, Scout (D. Appleton 1923)
Captain Jim Mason (D. Appleton 1924)
Mason and his Rangers (D. Appleton 1926)
Three Wilderness Scouts (D. Appleton 1930)

203. McALLISTER
By Matt Chisholm
Rem McAllister's adventures, penned by Peter Christopher Watts under a pseudonym, were issued in England and in the United States by Ballantine and Beagle.
The Hard Men (Mayflower 1963)
Death at Noon (Mayflower 1963)
The Hangman Rides Tall (Mayflower 1963) (Beagle 1971)
Kowa (Panther 1967)
Tough to Kill (Panther 1968)
Rage of McAllister (Panther 1969) (Beagle 1971)
McAllister Strikes (Panther 1969) (Beagle 1971)
Kill McAllister (Panther 1969) (Beagle 1972)
McAllister Rides (Panther 1969) (Beagle 1971)
McAllister Makes War (Panther 1969) (Beagle 1971)
McAllister's Fury (Panther 1969) (Beagle 1971)
McAllister Fights (Panther 1969) (Beagle 1971)
Gunsmoke for McAllister (Panther 1969) (Beagle 1970) (Ballantine)
McAllister (Ballantine)
McAllister Justice (Ballantine)
Blood on McAllister (Panther 1969) (Beagle 1970) (Ballantine)
McAllister Says No (Panther 1970) (Beagle 1971)
Danger for McAllister (Panther 1970)
McAllister Gambles (Panther 1970) (Beagle 1971)
Hang McAllister (Panther 1970) (Beagle 1970)
Shoot McAllister (Panther 1970) (Beagle 1971)
Hell for McAllister (Beagle)
Trail of McAllister (Panther 1970) (Beagle 1971)
McAllister Runs Wild (Mayflower 1972)
Brand McAllister (Mayflower 1972)
Battle of McAllister (Mayflower 1972)
McAllister Trapped (Mayflower 1973)
Vengeance of McAllister (Mayflower 1973)
McAllister Must Die (Mayflower 1974)
The McAllister Legend (Mayflower 1974)
McAllister Never Surrenders (Hamlyn 1981)
McAllister and Cheyenne Death (Hamlyn 1981)
McAllister and the Spanish Gold (Hamlyn 1981)
McAllister on the Comanche Crossing (Hamlyn 1981)
McAllister and Quarry (Hamlyn 1981)
Die-Hard (Hamlyn 1981)
Wolf-Bait (Hamlyn 1981)
Fire-Brand (Hamlyn 1981)

MANHUNTER
See KERSHAW

PAGE MARSHALL
See MURDOCK

204. RUSH McCOWAN
By Robert Bell
Historical detail is woven into this series.
Feud at Devil's River (Ballantine 1982)
Platte River Crossing (Ballantine 1983)
To the Death (Ballantine 1984)

205. BUCKSHOT McGEE
By Lee Floren
Buck McGee and Tortilla Joe are saddlepards who share Western exploits. Some of the novels were originally issued in hardcover. The characters also appeared in short stories in the pulps.
Wyoming Gun Law (Lancer 1967)
Shootout at Milk River (Milk River Range) (Belmont 1971)
The Saddle Tramps (Manor 1977)
Powder-Smoke Lawyer (Manor 1979)
Riders of Death (Cottonwoods Pards) (Unibooks no date)

206. JED McLANE
By Donald Honig
The protagonist is a young man in this juvenile series.
Adventures of Jed McLane
Jed McLane and the Storm Cloud (Dell)
Jed McLane and the Stranger (Dell 1976)

207. THE MEDICO
By James L. Rubel
Dr. Monroe is featured in these books.
The Medico of Painted Springs (Phoenix Press 1934) (Mills and Boon 1935)
The Medico Rides (Phoenix Press 1935) (Mills and Boon 1936)
The Medico on the Trail (Phoenix Press 1938) (Ward Lock 1939)

MEN FROM SHILOH
See VIRGINIAN

208. MEXICAN WAR SERIES
By Capt. Ralph Bonehill
Edward Stratemeyer wrote this boys' book series.
For the Liberty of Texas (Dana Estes 1900)
With Taylor on the Rio Grande (Dana Estes 1901)
Under Scott in Mexico (Dana Estes 1902)

209. MONTANA
By Al Cody
Montana Abbott's adventures were written pseudonymously by Archie
L. Joscelyn. Many are reprinted from hardcover.
The Ranch at Powder River (Manor 1972)
Broken Wheels (Manor 1973)
East to Montana (Manor 1974)
Iron Horse Country (Manor 1974)
Montana's Golden Gamble (Manor 1976)
Gun Song at Twilight (Manor 1976)
The Texan from Montana (Manor 1976)
The Tail Dies at Sundown (Manor 1976)
Montana's Territory (Manor 1976)
The Three McMahons (Manor 1977)

210. MONTANA KID
By Evan Evans
Montana — called El Keed by the Mexicans — was written by Frederick
Faust (Max Brand) under this penname. The books were first published
in the pulps, then hardcover, and then were re-issued in several paper-
back editions.
Montana Rides (Harper 1933) (Penguin 1957)
Montana Rides Again (Harper 1934)
Song of the Whip (Harper 1936) (Cassell 1936)

211. CONNIE MORGAN
By James B. Hendryx
This is a boys' book series.
Connie Morgan in Alaska (G.P. Putnam's 1916) (Jarrolds 1919)
Connie Morgan with the Mounted (G.P. Putnam's 1918) (Jarrolds 1924)
Connie Morgan in the Lumber Camps (G.P. Putnam's 1919) (Jarrolds
1928)
Connie Morgan in the Fur Country (G.P. Putnam's 1921) (Jarrolds
1928)
Connie Morgan in the Cattle Country (G.P. Putnam's 1923) (Jarrolds
1927)
Connie Morgan with the Forest Rangers (G.P. Putnam's 1925) (Jarrolds
1926)
Connie Morgan, Prospector (G.P. Putnam's 1929) (Jarrolds 1930)
Connie Morgan Hits the Trail (G.P. Putnam's 1929)
Connie Morgan in the Arctic (G.P. Putnam's 1936)
Connie Morgan in the Barren Lands (G.P. Putnam's 1937)

212. DRIFTER MORGAN
By Matt Weston
This cowboy wears a patch over his bad eye. The author is Howard
Pehrson.
Morgan (Paperback Library 1970)

2. Morgan's Revenge (Paperback Library 1971)

213. MORGETTE
By G.G. Boyer
Dolf Morgette is a gunman in books written by Glenn G. Boyer.
The Guns of Morgette (Walker 1982)
Morgette in the Yukon (Walker 1983)
Morgette on the Barbary Coast (Walker 1984)
Return of Morgette (Walker 1985)

214. MOUNTAIN GIRL
By Genevieve May Fox
This is a girls' book series.
Mountain Girl (Little 1932)
Mountain Girl Comes Home (Little 1934)
Lona of Hollybush Creek (Little 1935)

215. MOUNTAIN PONY
By Henry V. Larom
Andy Marvin went West to visit his Uncle Wes Marvin and Wes's
adopted daughter Sally in the Rocky Mountains and ended up having a
number of adventures with the sorrel horse Sunny.
Mountain Pony (Whittlesey House)
Mountain Pony and the Pinto Colt (Whittlesey House)
Mountain Pony and the Rodeo Mystery (Whittlesey House)
Mountain Pony and the Elkhorn Mystery (Whittlesey House 1950)

216. MOUNTAIN STANDARD TIME TRILOGY
By Paul Horgan
The works were collected in an omnibus volume.
Main Line West (Harper 1936)
Far From Cibola (Harper 193)
The Common Heart (Harper 1942)
Mountain Standard Time (trilogy) (Farrar Straus 1962)

217. THE MOUNTIES
By Terrence Dicks
The series spotlights Rob MacGregor of Canada's national police force.
The Mounties — The Great March West (Target 1976)
The Mounties — Massacre in the Hills (Target 1976)
The Mounties — Wardrums of the Blackfoot (Target)

218. MULVANE
By William Heuman
The hero is an Irishman.
Then Came Mulvane (Avon 1959)
Bullets for Mulvane (Avon 1960)
Mulvane's War (Avon 1960)

Mulvane on the Prod (Avon 1962)

219. PAGE MURDOCK
By Loren D. Estleman
Deputy Page Murdock's name was changed to Marshall for the Pocket
edition of the first entry, then switched back for the second. Fawcett
reprinted later entries.
The High Rocks (Doubleday 1979)
Stamping Ground (Doubleday 1980)
Murdock's Law (Doubleday 1982)
The Stranglers (Doubleday 1984)

220. MUSKET BOYS
By George A. Warren
This is a boys' book series.
The Musket Boys of Old Boston or, The First Blow for Liberty (Cupples
and Leon 1909)
The Musket Boys Under Washington or, The Tories of Old New York
(Cupples and Leon 1909)
The Musket Boys on the Delaware or, A Stirring Victory at Trenton
(Cupples and Leon 1910)

221. MUSTANG MARSHAL
By Burt Arthur
These books were written by Herbert A. Shappiro.
The Black Rider (Arcadia House 1941)
The Valley of Death (Arcadia House 1941)
Chenago Pass (Arcadia House 1942)

222. NARRATIVES OF AMERICA
By Allan W. Eckert
These massive sagas are well-grounded in historical detail, and include
indexes, though they are fiction. They were reprinted in paper by Ban-
tam. In hardcover they were called the Winning of America series.
The Frontiersmen (Little Brown 1967)
Wilderness Empire (Little Brown 1969)
The Conquerors (Little Brown 1970)
The Wilderness War (Little Brown 1978)
Gateway (Little Brown 1983)

223. LARAMIE NELSON
By Zane Grey and Romer Zane Grey
The hero of Zane Grey's *Riders of Spanish Peaks* was revived for a series
of novelettes in *Zane Grey's Western Magazine*. They were collected in
book form by Tower, then reprinted by Leisure.
Raiders of the Spanish Peaks by Zane Grey (Harper 1938)
Laramie Nelson: The Other Side of the Canyon by Romer Zane Grey

(Tower 1980) (Ian Henry 1986)
Laramie Nelson: The Lawless Land by Romer Zane Grey (Leisure 1984)

224. NEVADA JIM
By Marshall Grover
The Big Jim Rand series by Marshall Grover (actually Leonard F. Mears) first appeared in Australia. For U.S. publication, the hero became Big Jim Gage, and the author was Marshall McCoy. His U.S. books were printed with cover art and format similar to the then-popular Doc Savage pulp reprints from the same house (Bantam).
The Night McLennan Died (Scripts 1964)
Meet Me in Moredo (Scripts)
One Man Jury (Scripts)
The Valiant Die First (Scripts)
The Hour Before Disaster (Scripts)
No Escape Trail (Scripts)
The Man Who Hunts Jenner (Scripts)
One Thousand Dollar Target (Scripts)
Canyon Vigil (Scripts)
Gun Trapped (Scripts)
Main Street, Gallego (Scripts)
Devil's Legend (Scripts)
League of the Lawless (Scripts)
The Name on the Bullet (Scripts)
Vengeance is a Bullet (Scripts)
Wear Black for Johnny (Scripts)
Vigil on Boot Hill (Scripts)
They Came to Plunder (Scripts)
Diary of a Desperado (Scripts)
The Killers Wore Black (Scripts)
Satan Pulled the Trigger (Scripts)
Wear the Star Proudly (Scripts)
Thirty Raiders South (Scripts)
Guns of Greed (Scripts)
Die Lonesome (Scripts)
Kid Wichita (Scripts)
Shadow of a Colt .45 (Scripts)
Seven Westbound (Scripts)
Diablo's Shadow (Scripts 1967)
Kid Daybreak (Scripts 1967)
A Man Called Drago (Scripts 1967) (Bantam)
Six Rogues Riding (Scripts 1967)
Vengeance Rides a Black Horse (Scripts 1967)
Big Lobo (Scripts 1967) (Bantam)
Challenge of the Guilty (Scripts 1967)
Driscoll (Scripts 1967)
Fury at Broken Wheel (Scripts 1967)

Limbo Pass (Scripts 1967) (Bantam)
No Gun Is Neutral (Scripts 1968) (Bantam)
Seven Westbound (Bantam)
Bury the Guilty (Horwitz 1968) (Bantam 1968)
Justice for Jenner (Horwitz 1968) (Bantam 1968)
Crisis at Cornerstone (Horwitz 1968)
Die Brave (Horwitz 1968) (Bantam)
Gun Flash (Horwitz 1969) (Bantam)
Guns of Greed (Bantam)
Hangrope Fever (Horwitz 1969)
Killer Bait (Horwitz 1969) (Bantam)
Requiem for Sam Wade (Horwitz 1969)
Spur Route (Horwitz 1969)
Behind the Black Mask (Horwitz 1969) (Bantam 1969)
Bounty on Wes Durand (Horwitz 1969) (Bantam 1969)
Satan's Back Trail (Horwitz 1969) (Bantam 1969)
The Killers Came at Noon (Bantam)
Crisis at Cornerstone (Bantam)
Danger Rode Drag (Horwitz 1970)
Dead Man's Bluff (Horwitz 1970)
Rogue Trail (Horwitz 1970)
Stand Alone (Horwitz 1970)
Sundance Creek (Horwitz 1970)
The Willing Target (Horwitz 1970)
Sarson's Bonanza (Horwitz 1970)
Day of Vengeance (Horwitz 1970)
Gun Sinister (Horwitz 1971)
Gunfight at Doone's Well (Horwitz 1971)
Ransom for a Redhead (Horwitz 1971)
No Tomorrow for Tobin (Horwitz 1971)
San Saba Blockade (Horwitz 1972)
Hartigan (Horwitz 1972)
Savage Sunday (Horwitz 1972)

NORTHLAND SERIES
See DICK KENT

225. NORTHWEST STORIES
By Various Authors
This is a boys' book series. The seventh and eighth entries are reprints from the publishers Adventure Stories for Boys Series.
The Lead Disk by Leroy Snell (Cupples and Leon 1934)
The Shadow Patrol by Snell (Cupples and Leon 1934)
The Wolf Cry by Snell (Cupples and Leon 1934)
The Spirit of the North by Snell (Cupples and Leon 1935)
The Challenge of the Yukon by Snell (Cupples and Leon 1935)
The Phantom of the Rivers by Snell (Cupples and Leon 1936)

Sergeant Dick by J.G. Rowe (Cupples and Leon 1929)
The Carcajou by Rowe (Cupples and Leon 1931)
Danger Trails North by Billy L. Bennett (Cupples and Leon 1936)

226. NORTHWEST TERRITORY
By Oliver Payne
This saga series was put together by Book Creations Inc. for Berkley.
1. Warpath (Berkley 1982)
2. Conquest (Berkley 1982)
3. Defiance (Berlkey 1984)
4. Conflict (Berkley 1984)
5. Rebellion (Berkley 1984)
6. Triumph (Berkley 1985)
7. Betrayal (Berkley 1986)

227. NOVELS OF THE AMERICAN FRONTIER
By Janice Holt Giles
This saga series was reprinted in paperback by Warner. It features the
Fowler family through several generations.
The Kentuckians (Houghton Mifflin 1953)
Hannah Fowler (Houghton Mifflin 1956)
The Believers (Houghton Mifflin 1957)
Johnny Osage (Houghton Mifflin 1960)
Savanna (Houghton Mifflin 1961)
Voyage to Santa Fe (Houghton Mifflin 1962)
The Great Adventure (Houghton Mifflin 1967)
The Land Beyond the Mountains (Warner)
Run Me A River (Warner)

O'BRIEN
See BUFFALO HUNTER

228. OLD SHATTERHAND
By Karl May
Three books, originally published in Germany, feature Old Shatterhand
and his companion Winnetou.
Winnetou (1893)
Old Surehand (1894)
Winnetou's Heritage (1910)

229. ORDE FAMILY
By Stewart Edward White
These are frontier stories.
The Blazed Trail (McClure 1902) (Constable 1902)
The Riverman (McClure 1908) (Hodder & Stoughton 1908)
The Adventures of Bobby Orde (Doubleday 1911) (Unwin 1912) Bobby Orde (Hodder & Stoughton 1916)
The Rules of the Game (Doubleday 1910) (Nelson 1911)

230. ELFEGO O'REILLY
By Alex Hawk
While the publisher issued many books under this house name, only one
entry was located identified as "An Elfego O'Reilly Western" and featur-
ing the half-Mexican, half-Irish-American.
Half-Breed (Popular Library 1971)

231. WILDCAT O'SHEA
By Jeff Clinton
Jack M. Bickham pseudonymously penned this humorous series about a
red-haired cowboy. Some entries were also published in large-type edi-
tions.
Fighting Buckaroo (Berkley 1961)
Wildcat's Rampage (Berkley 1962)
Wildcat Against the House (Berkley 1963)
Wildcat's Revenge (Berkley 1964)
Wildcat Takes His Medicine (Berkley 1966)
Wanted: Wildcat O'Shea (Berkley 1967)
Wildcat on the Loose (Berkley 1967)
Wildcat's Witch Hunt (Berkley 1967)
Watch Out for Wildcat (Berkley 1968
Wildcat Meets Miss Melody (Berkley 1968)
Build a Box for Wildcat (Berkley 1969)
A Stranger Named O'Shea (Berkley 1970)
Bounty on Wildcat (Berkley 1971)
Wildcat's Claim to Fame (Berkley 1971)
Hang High, O'Shea (Berkley 1972)

232. MOLLY OWENS
By Stephen Overholser
Molly Owens is an ace operative for the Fenton Investigative Agency in
this adult series.
1. Molly and the Gold Baron (Bantam 1981)
2. Molly on the Outlaw Trail (Bantam 1982)
3. Molly and the Indian Agent (Bantam 1982)
4. Molly and the Railroad Tycoon (Bantam 1983)
5. Molly and the Gambler (Bantam 1984)

PAINTED POST
See SHERIFF BLUE STEELE

233. PAINTIN' PISTOLEER
By Walker A. Tompkins
The stories of Justin Other Smith were originally a series in *Zane Grey's
Western Magazine*. The hero is both a calendar artist and top six-gun ar-
tist in Arizona Territory.
The Paintin' Pistoleer (Dell 1949)

PALADIN
  See HAVE GUN, WILL TRAVEL

234. AL PALMER
  By Edward H. Hawkins
  Palmer is a U.S. Marshal in Dakota Territory. This was announced as the first book in a series.
  Prisoner of Devil's Claw (Apollo Books 1971)

235. RIDGE PARKMAN
  By Greg Hunt
  The hero is an outlaw.
  Ride to Vengeance (Dell 1980)
  DeWitt's Strike (Dell 1980)
  When Legends Die (Dell 1982)
  The Havens Raid (Dell 1980)
  Mission to Darkness (Dell 1983)

PATHFINDER
  See DEERSLAYER

236. PATTY LOU
  By Basil Miller
  This is a girls' book series.
  Patty Lou of the Golden West (Zondervan 1942)
  Patty Lou and the White Gold Ranch (Zondervan 1943)
  Patty Lou's Pot of Gold (Zondervan 1943)
  Patty Lou in the Coast Guard (Zondervan 1944)
  Patty Lou, The Flying Nurse (Zondervan 1945)
  Patty Lou, The Girl Forester (Zondervan 1947)
  Patty Lou, Flying Missionary (Zondervan 1948)
  Patty Lou in the Wilds of Central America (Zondervan 1949)
  Patty Lou under Western Skies (Zondervan 1950)
  Patty Lou Home on the Range (Zondervan 1951)
  Patty Lou at Sunset Pass (Zondervan 1952)
  Patty Lou Lost in the Jungle (Zondervan 1953)
  Patty Lou, Range Nurse (Zondervan 1954)
  Patty Lou and the Seminole Indians (Zondervan 1955)

237. THE PEACEMAKER
  By William S. Brady
  This is a British paperback series.
  1.
  2.
  3. Whiplash (by John B. Harvey) (Fontana 1981)

PINKERTON SERIES
  See RAIDER AND DOC

238. PIONEER BOYS
By Harrison L. Adams
St. George Rathbone wrote this boys' book series.
The Pioneer Boys of the Ohio or, Clearing the Wilderness (L.C. Page 1912)
The Pioneer Boys on the Great Lakes or, On the Trail of the Iroquois (L.C. Page 1912)
The Pioneer Boys of the Mississippi or, The Homestead in the Wilderness (L.C. Page 1913)
The Pioneer Boys of the Missouri or, In the Country of the Sioux (L.C. Page 1914)
The Pioneer Boys of the Yellowstone or, Lost in the Land of Wonders (L.C. Page 1915)
The Pioneer Boys of the Columbia or, In the Wilderness of the Great Northwest (L.C. Page 1916)
The Pioneer Boys of the Colorado or, Braving the Perils of the Grand Canyon Country (L.C. Page 1926)
The Pioneer Boys of Kansas or, A Prairie Home in Buffalo Land (L.C. Page 1928)

239. PIONEER SCOUT SERIES
By Everett T. Tomlinson
This is a boys' book series.
Scouting with Daniel Boone (Doubleday, Page 1914)
Scouting with Kit Carson (Doubleday, Page 1916)
Scouting with General Funston (Doubleday, Page 1917)
Scouting with General Pershing (Doubleday, Page 1918)

240. PONY GEORGE
By Clem Colt
Nelson Nye wrote these books.
Gun-Smoke (Greenburg 1938) as by Nelson Nye (Nicholson and Watson 1938)
The Shootin' Sheriff (Phoenix Press 1938) (Nicholson and Watson 1939)

241. PONY RIDER BOYS SERIES
By Frank Gee Patchin
This is a boys' book series.
The Pony Rider Boys in the Rockies or, The Secret of the Lost Claim (Henry Altemus 1909)
The Pony Rider Boys in Texas or, The Veiled Riddle of the Plains (Henry Altemus 1910)
The Pony Rider Boys in Montana or, The Mystery of the Old Custer Trail (Henry Altemus 1910)
The Pony Rider Boys in the Ozarks or, The Secret of Ruby Mountain (Henry Altemus 1910)
The Pony Rider Boys in the Alkali or, Finding the Key to the Desert

Maze (Henry Altemus 1910)
    The Pony Rider Boys in New Mexico or, The End of the Silver Trail
(Henry Altemus 1910)
    The Pony Rider Boys in the Grand Canyon or, The Mystery of Bright
Angel Gulch (Henry Altemus 1912)
    The Pony Rider Boys with the Texas Rangers or, On The Trail of the
Border Bandits (Henry Altemus 1920)
    The Pony Rider Boys on the Blue Ridge or, A Lucky Find in the
Carolina Mountains (Henry Altemus 1924)
    The Pony Rider Boys in New England or, An Exciting Quest in the
Maine Wilderness (Henry Altemus 1924)
    The Pony Rider Boys in Louisiana or, Following the Game Trails in the
Canebreak (Henry Altemus 1924)
    The Pony Rider Boys in Alaska or, The Gold Diggers of Taku Pass
(Henry Altemus 1924)

242. POWDER VALLEY
    By Peter Field
This is one of the longer running hardcover and paperback Western
series. Books were issued in hardcover first by Morrow, later by Jeffer-
son House. They were reprinted by Pocket, Bantam and Armed Services
Editions. The books feature Pat Stevens and his pals Sam Sloan and
Ezra. Eleven writers contributed to the house series over the years. The
first entry was printed in the November-December 1933 issue of
Western Story Magazine.
    Outlaws Three (by Francis Thayer Hobson) (Morrow 1934)
    Dry Gulch Adams (by Hobson) (Morrow 1934)
    Gringo Guns (by Hobson) (Morrow 1935)
    Boss of the Lazy 9 (by E.B. Mann) (Morrow 1936)
    Coyote Gulch (by Samuel Mines) (Morrow 1936)
    Mustang Mesa (by Ed Earl Repp) (Morrow1937)
    Canyon of Death (by Harry Sinclair Drago) (Morrow 1938)
    Outlaw of Eagle's Nest (by S. Lancer Cheney) (Morrow 1938)
    Tenderfoot Kid (by Drago) (Morrow 1939)
    Doctor Two-Guns (by Drago) (Morrow 1939)
    Law Badge (by Drago) (Morrow 1940)
    Man from Thief River (by Drago) (Morrow 1940)
    Guns from Powder Valley (by Davis Dresser) (Morrow 1941)
    Powder Valley Pay-Off (by Dresser) (Morrow 1941)
    Fight for Powder Valley (by Dresser) (Morrow 1942) The Land Grab-
ber (Bantam 1949)
    Law Man of Powder Valley (by Dresser) (Morrow 1942)
    Trail South from Powder Valley (by Dresser) (Morrow 1942)
    Sheriff on the Spot (by Dresser) (Morrrow 1943)
    Powder Valley Vengeance (by Dresser) (Jefferson House 1943)
    Death Rides the Night (by Dresser) (Jefferson House 1944)
    Smoking Iron (by Dresser) (Jefferson House 1944)
    Maverick's Return (by Dresser) (Jefferson House 1944)

Midnight Roundup (by Dresser) (Jefferson House 1944)
End of the Trail (by Dresser) (Jefferson House 1945)
Road to Laramie (by Dresser) (Jefferson House 1945)
Gambler's Gold (by Fred East) (Jefferson House 1946)
Powder Valley Showdown (by Dresser) (Jefferson Hose 1946)
Ravaged Range (by East) (Jefferson House 1946)
Trail from Needle Rock (by East) (Jefferson House 1947)
Return to Powder Valley (by Robert J. Hogan) (Jefferson House 1948)
Outlaw Valley (by Hogan) (Jefferson House 1948)
Sheriff Wanted (by Hogan) (Jefferson House 1949)
Sheriff's Revenge (Bantam 1949)
Hell's Corner (Bantam 1950)
Blacksnake Trail (by Hogan) (Jefferson House 1950)
Powder Valley Ambush (by Lucien W. Emerson) (Jefferson House 1950)
Back Trail to Danger (by Emerson) (Jefferson House 1951)
Canyon Hide-Out (by Emerson) (Jefferson House 1951)
Law Badge (by Emerson) (Jefferson House 1951)
Marauders at the Lazy Mare (by Emerson) (Jefferson House 1951)
Guns in the Saddle (by Emerson) (Jefferson House 1952)
Powder Valley Holdup (by Emerson) (Jefferson House 1952)
Riders of the Outlaw Trail (by Emerson) (Jefferson House 1952)
Three Guns from Colorado (by Emerson) (Jefferson House 1952)
Canyon of Death (by Emerson) (Jefferson House 1952)
Dig the Spurs Deep (by Emerson) (Jefferson House 1953)
Guns Roaring West (by Emerson) (Jefferson House 1953)
Montana Maverick (by Emerson) (Jefferson House 1953)
Maverick's Return (by Emerson) (Jefferson House 1954)
Powder Valley Deadlock (by Emerson) (Jefferson House 1954)
Powder Valley Stampede (by Emerson) (Jefferson House 1954)
Ride for Trinidad (by Emerson) (Jefferson House 1954)
War in the Painted Buttes (by Emerson) (Jefferson House 1954)
Rawhide Rider (by Emerson) (Jefferson House 1955)
Saddles to Santa Fe (by Emerson) (Jefferson House 1955)
Breakneck Pass (by Emerson) (Jefferson House 1955)
Outlaw of Castle Canyon (by Emerson) (Jefferson House 1955)
Strike for Tomahawk (by Emerson) (Jefferson House 1956)
Powder Valley Renegade (by Emerson) (Jefferson Hose 1956)
Wild Horse Lightning (by Emerson) (Jefferson House 1956)
Guns for Grizzley Flat (by Emerson) (Jefferson House 1957)
Man from Robber's Roost (by Emerson) (Jefferson House 1957)
Powder Valley Manhunt (by Emerson) (Jefferson House 1957)
Raiders at Medicine Bow (by Emerson) (Jefferson House 1957)
Hangman's Trail (by Emerson) (Jefferson House 1958)
Rustler's Rock (by Emerson) (Jefferson House 1958)
Sagebrush Swindle (by Emerson) (Jefferson House 1958)
Drive for Devil's River (by Emerson) (Jefferson House 1959)
Outlaw Express (by Emerson) (Jefferson House 1959)

Trail to Troublesome (by Emerson) (Jefferson House 1959)
Double-Cross Canyon (by Emerson) (Jefferson House 1960)
Powder Valley Plunder (by Emerson) (Jefferson House 1960)
Rattlesnake Range (by Emerson) (Jefferson House 1961)
Wolf Pack Trail (by Emerson) (Jefferson House 1961)
Rimrock Riders (by Emerson) (Jefferson House 1961)
Cougar Canyon (by Emerson) (Jefferson House 1962)
The Outlaw Herd (by Emerson) (Jefferson House 1962)
Powder Valley Ransom (by Emerson) (Jefferson House 1962)
Trail Through Toscosa (by Emerson) (Jefferson House 1963)
Powder Valley Getaway (by Emerson) (Jefferson House 1963)
Rustler's Empire (by Emerson) (Jefferson House 1964)
Feud at Silvermine (by Emerson) (Jefferson House 1965)
Outlaw Deputy (by Emerson) (Pocket 1967)

243. PRAIRIE ROMANCE
By Janette Oke
Inspirational romances involve the Davis family.
  Love Comes Softly (Bethany House 1979)
  Love's Enduring Promise (Bethany House 1980)
  Love's Long Journey (Bethany House 1982)
  Love's Abiding Joy (Bethany House 1983)
  Love's Unending Legacy (Bethany House 1984)

244. QUICKSILVER
By Amos Moore
These are formulary Westerns.
  Quicksilver (Washburn 1936) Quicksilver Rides (Harrap 1936)
  Quicksilver Justice (Harrap 1936)

245. GREGORY QUIST
By William Colt MacDonald
Quist is featured in the Railroad Detective Series, in hardcover and soft-bound editions.
  Law and Order, Unlimited (Doubleday 1953) (Hodder and Stoughton 1955)
  Mascarada Pass (Doubleday 1954) (Hodder and Stoughton 1957)
  The Comanche Scalp (Lippincott 1955) (Hodder and Stoughton 1958)
  Destination Danger (Lippincott 1955) (Hodder and Stoughton 1957)
Whiplash (Ulverscroft 1979)
  The Devil's Drum (Lippincott 1956) (Hodder and Stoughton 1962)
Hellgate (Belmont 1978)
  Action at Arcanum (Lippincott 1958) (Hodder and Stoughton 1961)
  Tombstone for a Troubleshooter (Lippincott 1960) Hodder and Stoughton 1961) Trouble Shooter (Berkley 1965)
  The Osage Bow (Hodder and Stoughton 1964)
  Incident at Horcado City (Belmont Tower 1969) (Henry 1979)

246. RAIDER AND DOC
  By J.D. Hardin
This adult series, initially called the Pinkerton Series, is about two Western detectives. Berkley picked up the series, and reprinted earlier entries when Playboy folded.
  The Good, The Bad and The Deadly (Playboy 1979)
  Blood, Sweat and Gold (Playboy 1979)
  The Slick and the Dead (Playboy 1979)
  Bullets, Buzzards, Boxes of Pine (Playboy 1980)
  Face Down in a Coffin (Playboy 1980)
  The Man Who Bit Snakes (Playboy 1980)
  The Spirit and the Flesh (Playboy 1980)
  Bloody Sands (Playboy 1980)
  Raider's Hell (Playboy 1980)
  Raider's Revenge (Playboy 1981)
  Hard Chains, Soft Women (Playboy 1981)
  Raider's Gold (Playboy 1981)
  Silver Tombstones (Playboy 1981)
  Death Lode (Playboy 1981)
  Coldhearted Lady (Playboy 1981)
  Gunfire at Spanish Rock (Playboy 1982)
  Sons and Sinners (Playboy 1982)
  Death Flotilla (Playboy 1982)
  Snake River Rescue (Playboy 1982)
  The Lone Star Massacre (Playboy 1982)
  Bobbles, Baubles and Blood (Playboy 1982)
  Bibles, Bullets and Brides (Berkley 1983)
  Hellfire Hideaway (Berkley 1983)
  Apache Gold (Berkley 1983)
  Saskatchewan Rising (Berkley 1983)
  Hangman's Noose (Berkley 1983)
  Bloody Time in Blacktower (Berkley 1983)
  The Man with No Face (Berkley 1983)
  The Firebrands (Berkley 1983)
  Downriver to Hell (Berkley 1983)
  Bounty Hunter (Berkley 1983)
  Queens Over Deuces (Berkley 1984)
  Carnival of Death (Berkley 1984)
  Satan's Bargain (Berkley 1984)
  The Wyoming Special (Berkley 1984)
  Lead-Lined Coffins (Berkley 1984)
  San Juan Shootout (Berkley 1984)
  The Pecos Dollars (Berkley 1984)
  Vengeance Valley (Berkley 1984)
  Outlaw Trail (Berkley 1984)
  Homesteader's Revenge (Berkley 1984)
  Tombstone in Deadwood (Berkley 1984)
  The Rawhiders (Berkley 1984)

Colorado Silver Queen (Berkley 1985)
The Buffalo Soldiers (Berkley 1985)
The Great Jewel Robbery (Berkley 1985)
Ozark Outlaws (Berkley 1985)
The Cochise County War (Berkley 1985)
Apache Trail (Berkley 1985)
In the Heart of Texas (Berkley 1985)
The Colorado Sting (Berkley 1985)
Hell's Belle (Berkley 1985)
Cattletown War (Berkley 1985)
The Ghost Mine (Berkley 1985)
Maximilian's Gold (Berley 1985)
The Tincup Railroad War (Berkley 1985)
Carson City Colt (Berkley 1986)
Guns at Buzzard Bend (Berkley 1986)
The Runaway Rancher (Berkley 1986)
The Longest Manhunt (Berkley 1986)
The Northland Marauders (Berkley 1986)

RAILROAD DETECTIVE SERIES
  See QUIST

247. RAILROADS ACROSS AMERICA
  By G.J. Morgan
The title was announced as the first in a series.
  Hell on Wheels (Futura 1975)

248. JIM RAINEY
  By Peter McCurtin
This is a formulary series.
  Spoils of War (Belmont 1976) (New English Library 1978)
  Ambush at Derati Wells (Belmont 1977) (New English Library 1978)
  First Blood (Belmont 1977) (New English Library 1978)

249. HEC RAMSEY
  By Various Authors
Ramsey appeared on an American television series 1972-74.
  Hec Ramsey by Dean Owen (Award)
  Hec Ramsey: The Hunted by Joe Millard (Award 1974)

250. RANCH GIRLS
  By Margaret Vandercook
This is a girls' book series.
  The Ranch Girls at Rainbow Lodge (Winston 1911)
  The Ranch Girls' Pot of Gold (Winston 1912)
  The Ranch Girls at Boarding School (Winston 1913)
  The Ranch Girls in Europe (Winston 1913)
  The Ranch Girls at Home Again (Winston 1915)

The Ranch Girls and Their Great Adventure (Winston 1917)
The Ranch Girls and Their Heart's Desire (Winston 1920)
The Ranch Girls and the Silver Arrow (Winston 1921)
The Ranch Girls and the Mystery of the Three Roads (Winston 1924)

251. RANCH AND RANGE
By St. George Rathbone
This is a juvenile series.
Sunset Ranch (Street & Smith 1902)
Chums of the Prairie (Street & Smith 1902)
The Young Range Riders (Street & Smith 1902)

252. RANCHO BRAVO
By Thorne Douglas
Ben L. Haas penned this series featuring a different member of the group in each title: Calhoon, Killraine, Gannon and Whitton.
Calhoon (Fawcett 1972)
The Big Drive (Fawcett 1973)
Killraine (Fawcett 1975)
Night Riders (Fawcett 1975)
The Mustang Men (Fawcett 1977)

253. RANGE AND GRANGE HUSTLERS
By Frank Gee Patchin
This is a boys' book series.
The Range and Grange Hustlers on the Ranch or, The Boy Shepherds of the Great Divide (Henry Altemus 1912)
The Range and Grange Hustlers' Greatest Roundup or, Pitting Their Wits Against a Packer's Combine (Henry Altemus 1912)
The Range and Grange Hustlers on the Plains or, Following the Steam Plows Across the Prairies (Henry Altemus 1913)
The Range and Grange Hustlers at Chicago or, The Conspiracy of the Wheat Pit (Henry Altemus 1913)

254. RAWHIDE RAWLINS
By Charles M. Russell
These are short story collections by the American painter and sculptor.
Rawhide Rawlins Stories (Montana Newspaper Association 1921)
More Rawhides (Montana Newspaper Association 1925)
Trails Plowed Under (omnibus) (Doubleday 1927) (Heinemann 1927)
Rawhide Rawlins Rides Again; or, Behind the Swinging Doors: A Collection of Charlie Russell's Favorite Stories (Trail's End 1948)

255. RED GAP
By Harry Leon Wilson
The first book was made into a motion picture.
Ruggles of Red Gap (Doubleday 1915) (Lane 1917)
Somewhere in Red Gap (Doubleday 1919) (Lane 1919)

256. RED PLUME
By Edward Huntington Williams
These are boys' book stories.
Red Plume (Harper 1925)
Red Plume Returns (Harper 1927)
Red Plume with the Royal Northwest Mounted (Harper 1927)

257. REEL WEST
Edited by Bill Pronzini and Martin H. Greenberg
The books feature short stories which were made into motion pictures.
Reel West (Dubleday 1984)
Second Reel West (Doubleday 1985)

258. RENEGADE
By Ramsay Thorne
Lou Cameron penned at least the first in this series. Captain Gringo, the
hero, is a soldier of fortune.
 1. Renegade (by Lou Cameron) (Warner 1979)
 2. Blood Runner (Warner 1979)
 3. Fear Merchant (Warner 1980)
 4. Death Hunter (Warner 1980)
 5. Macumba Killer (Warner 1980)
 6. Panama Gunner (Warner 1980)
 7. Death in High Places (Warner 1981)
 8. Over the Andes to Hell (Warner 1981)
 9. Hell Raider (Warner 1981)
10. The Great Game (Warner)
11. Citadel of Death (Warner)
12. The Badlands Brigade (Warner)
13. Mahogany Pirates (Warner 1982)
14. Harvest of Death (Warner 1982)
15. Terror Trail (Warner 1982)
16. Mexican Marauder (Warner 1983)
17. Slaughter in Sinaloa (Warner 1983)
18. Cavern of Doom (Warner 1983)
19. Hellfire in Honduras (Warner 1983)
20. Shots at Sunrise (Warner 1983)
21. River of Revenge (Warner 1983)
22. Payoff in Panama (Warner 1983)
23. Volcano of Violence (Warner 1984)
24. Guatemala Gunman (Warner 1984)
25. High Sea Showdown (Warner 1984)
26. Blood on the Border (Warner 1984)
27. Savage Safari (Warner 1984)
28. The Slave Raiders (Warner 1984)
29. Murder in Merida (Warner 1985)
30. Mayhem at Mission Bay (Warner 1985)
31. Shootout in Segovia (Warner 1985)

32. Death Over Darien (Warner 1985)
33. Costa Rican Carnage (Warner 1985)

259. RENFREW OF THE ROYAL MOUNTED
By Laurie Y. Erskine
The series features the Canadian crime fighting organization.
Renfrew of the Royal Mounted (D. Appleton 1922)
Renfrew Rides Again (D. Appleton 1927)
Renfrew Rides the Sky (D. Appleton 1928)
Renfrew Rides North (D. Appleton 1931)
Renfrew's Long Trail (D. Appleton 1933)
Renfrew Rides the Range (D. Appleton 1935)
Renfrew in the Valley of Vanished Men (D. Appleton 1936)
One Man Came Back (D. Appleton 1939)
Renfrew Flies Again (D. Appleton 1941)

260. REVOLUTIONARY SERIES
By Amy E. Blanchard
This is a girls' book series.
A Girl of '76 (Wilde 1898)
A Revolutionary Maid: A Story of the Middle Period of the War for Independence (Wilde 1899)
A Daughter of Freedom: A Story of the Latter Period of the War for Independence (Wilde 1900)
A Heroine of 1812: A Maryland Romance (Wilde 1901)
A Loyal Lass: A Story of the Niagara Campaign of 1814 (Wilde 1902)
A Gentle Pioneer: Being the Story of the Early Days in the New West (Wilde 1903)

261. RIM-FIRE
By Charles Ballew
The author is Charles H. Snow.
Rim-Fire, Detective (Wright and Brown 1936)
Rim-Fire on the Range (Wright and Brown 1936)
Rim-Fire, Sheriff (Wright and Brown 1936)
Rim-Fire Six Guns (Wright and Brown 1936)
Rim-Fire Fights (Wright and Brown 1937)
Rim-Fire Horns In (Wright and Brown 1937)
Rim-Fire, Ranchero (Wright and Brown 1937)
Rim-Fire Roams (Wright and Brown 1937)
Rim-Fire on the Desert (Wright and Brown 1938)
Rim-Fire Slips (Wright and Brown 1938)
Rim-Fire and Slats (Wright and Brown 1938)
Rim-Fire in Mexico (Wright and Brown 1939)
Rim-Fire Presides (Wright and Brown 1939)
Rim-Fire Runs (Wright and Brown 1941)
Rim-Fire Gets 'Em (Wright and Brown 1942)
Rim-Fire on the Prod (Wright and Brown 1944)

Rim-Fire Returns (Wright and Brown 1944)
Rim-Fire Skunked (Wright and Brown 1947)
Rim-Fire and the Bear (Wright and Brown 1950)
Rim-Fire Abstains (Wright and Brown 1953)

262. RIN TIN TIN
By Various Authors
The juvenile books are based on the 1954-59 American television series.
Rin Tin Tin's Rinty (Whitman 1954)
Rin Tin Tin and the Ghost Wagon Train (Whitman 1958)

263. THE RIO KID (I)
By Don Davis
Davis Dresser wrote this series, which was issued in paperback by
Pocket. The third entry was serialized in *Double-Action Western*.
Return of the Rio Kid (Morrow 1940) (Ward Lock 1950)
Death on Treasure Trail (Morrow 1941) (Hutchinson 1940)
Rio Kid Justice (Morrow 1941)
Two-Gun Rio Kid (Morrow 1941)

264. THE RIO KID (II)
By Various Authors
Bob Pryor, The Rio Kid, appeared originally in *The Rio Kid Western*, a
pulp fiction magazine which began in 1939. His adventures were record-
ed by several authors, some under their own names, some under
pseudonyms (Jackson Cole). The series was also reprinted in Great Bri-
tain. Historical figures frequently appear in the stories.
The Comstock Lode by Tom Curry (Curtis 1967)
The Rio Kid Rides Again by Curry (Curtis 1967)
Guns of the Sioux by Curry (Curtis 1968)
Pards of Buffalo Bill by Curry (Curtis 1968)
Riding for Custer by Curry (Curtis 1968) Frontier Massacre (Tandem
1974)
Storm over Yellowstone by C. William Harrison (Curtis 1968)
Kansas Marshal by Curry (Curtis 1968) (Tandem)
The Montana Vigilantes by Curry (Curtis 1969)
Arizona Blood by Curry (Curtis 1969)
Leadville Avengers by Curry (Curtis 1970)
Valley of Vanished Men by Harrison (Curtis 1970)
Hight Wire and Hot Lead by Harrison (Curtis 1970)
Kit Carson's Way by Curry (Curts 1970)
Guns of Dodge City by Curry (Curtis 1970)
Idaho Raiders by Curry (Curtis)
Lord of the Silver Lode by Lee E. Wells (Popular 1971)
King of Utah by Wells (Curtis)
Indian Outpost by Curry (Curtis 1971)
Wagons to California by Curry (Curtis 1972)
Border Patrol by Wells (Popular)

Sierra Gold by Wells (Popular)
Passport to Perdition by Gunnison Steele (Popular 1975)
On to Cheyenne by Wells (Popular)
Bugles on the Bighorn by Jackson Cole (Popular 1975)
Crown for Azora by Cole (Popular 1976)
The Trail of the Iron Horse by Walker A. Tompkins (Popular 1976)
Santa Fe Trail by Tompkins (Popular 1976)
Lion of the Lavabeds by Tompkins (Popular 1976)
Raiders of the Valley by Curry (Curtis 1976)
The Mormon Trail by Curry (Curtis)
The Stolen Empire by Curry (Curtis)
Riders of Steel by Curry (Curtis)
Golden Empire by Dean Owen (Curtis)

265. ROB RANGER SERIES
By Lt. Lionel Lounsberry
This is a boys' book series.
Rob Ranger's Mine or, The Boy Who Got There (Street & Smith 1903)
Rob Ranger the Young Ranchman or, Going It Alone At Lost River (Street & Smith 1903)
Rob Ranger's Cowboy Days or, The Young Hunter of the Big Horn (Street & Smith 1903)

266. ROCKABYE COUNTY
By J.T. Edson
The series is by the prolific British author.
The Professional Killers (Corgi 1968)
The ¼-second Draw (Corgi 1969)
The Deputies (Corgi 1969)
Point of Contact (Corgi 1970)
The Owlhoot (Corgi 1970)
Run for the Border (Corgi 1970)
Bad Hombre (Corgi 1971)
Sixteen-Dollar Shooter (Corgi 1974)
The Lawmen of Rockabye County (announced)
The Sheriff of Rockabye County (announced)

267. ROY ROGERS
By Various Authors
These books were about the B-Western movie star who married one of his leading ladies, Dale Evans.
Roy Rogers and the Gopher Creek Gunman by Don Middleton (Fran Striker) (Whitman 1945)
Roy Rogers and the Raiders of Sawtooth Ridge by Snowden Miller (Whitman 1946)
Roy Rogers and the Ghost of Mystery Ranch by Walker A. Tompkins (Whitman 1950)
Roy Rogers and the Outlaws of Sundown Valley by Miller (Whitman

1950)
Roy Rogers on the Double-R Ranch by Elizabeth Beecher (Simon and
Schuster 1951)
Roy Rogers and the Rimrock Renegade by Miller (Whitman 1952)
Roy Rogers and the Brasada Bandit (Whitman)
Roy Rogers and the Enchanged Canyon by Jim Rivers (Whitman 1954)
Roy Rogers, King of the Cowboys by Cole Fannin (Whitman 1956)
Roy Rogers and the Trail of Zeroes (Whitman)
Roy Rogers and Dale Evans: River of Peril (Whitman)
Dale Evans: Danger in Crooked Canyon (Whitman)

268. CHARITY ROSS
By Jack M. Bickham
The heroine is a young widow fighting to preserve her land in the first
book, and involved in a murder mystery in the second.
The War on Charity Ross (Doubleday 1967)
Target: Charity Ross (Doubleday 1968)

269. JOHNNY ROSS
By Dave Waldo
The writer is D. Waldo Clarke.
Beat the Drum Slowly (Ward Lock 1961)
No Man Rides Alone (Ward Lock 1965)
Once in the Saddle (Ward Lock 1968)

270. RED RYDER
By Various Authors
The series is based on Fred Harmon's newspaper comic strip, which was
made into a series of B-Western movies. Ryder and his sidekick Little
Beaver are featured.
Red Ryder and the Mystery of the Whispering Walls by R.R. Winter-
botham (Whitman 1941)
Red Ryder and the Secret of Wolf Canyon by S.S. Stevens (Whitman
1941)
Red Ryder and the Adventure at Chimney Rock by H.C. Thomas
(Whitman 1946)
Red Ryder and the Secret of the Lucky Mine by Carl W. Smith (Whit-
man 1947)
Red Ryder and the Riddle of Roaring Range by Jerry McGill (Whitman
1951)
Red Ryder and Gun-Smoke Gold by McGill (Whitman 1954)
Red Ryder and the Thunder Trail by McGill (Whitman 1956)

271. SABATA
By Brian Fox
This series is based on the motion picture featuring Lee Van Cleef. Writ-
ten by W.T. Ballard, they were first issued in England.

Sabata (Award 1970)
Return of Sabata (Award 1972)

272. SACKETTS
By Louis L'Amour
Different members of the Sackett clan are featured in this series of paperback originals. Some entries were later issued in hardcover by Saturday Review Press.
1. Sackett's Land (Bantam) (Saturday Review Press 1974) (Corgi 1975)
2. To the Far Blue Mountains (Bantam) (Saturday Review Press 1976) (Corgi 1977)
3. The Daybreakers (Bantam) (Tandem 1960) (Hammond 1964)
4. Sackett (Bantam 1961) (Hammond 1964)
5. Lando (Bantam 1962) (Corgi 1963)
6. Mojave Crossing (Bantam 1964) (Corgi 1964)
7. The Sackett Brand (Bantam 1965) (Corgi 1965)
8. The Lonely Men (Bantam 1969) (Corgi 1971)
9. Treasure Mountain (Bantam 1972) (Corgi 1973)
10. Mustang Man (Bantam 1966) (Corgi 1966)
11. Galloway (Bantam 1970) (Corgi 1970)
12. The Sky-Liners (Bantam 1967) (Corgi 1971)
13. The Man from the Broken Hills (Bantam 1975) (Corgi 1976)
14. Ride the Dark Trail (Bantam 1972) (Corgi 1972)
15. The Warrior's Path (Bantam 1980) (Corgi 1981)
16. Lonely on the Mountain (Bantam)
17. Ride the River (Bantam 1983)
18. Son of a Wanted Man (Bantam 1984)
Sackett's Gold (Bantam 1977)
19. Jubal Sackett (Bantam 1985)

273. SADDLE BOYS
By Capt. James Carson
This is a boys' book series.
The Saddle Boys of the Rockies or, Lost on Thunder Mountain (Cupples and Leon 1913)
The Saddle Boys in the Grand Canyon or, The Hermit of the Cave (Cupples and Leon 1913)
The Saddle Boys on the Plains or, After a Treasure of Gold (Cupples and Leon 1913)
The Saddle Boys at Circle Ranch or, In at the Grand Round-Up (Cupples and Leon 1913)
The Saddle Boys on Mexican Trails or, In the Hands of the Enemy (Cupples and Leon 1915)

274. JIM SADDLER
By Gene Curry
This is an adult Western series. See Carmody entry for more information.

1. A Dirty Way to Die (Tower 1979)
2. Wildcat Woman (Tower 1979)
3. Colorado Crossing (Tower 1979)
4. Hot as a Pistol (Tower 1980)
5. Wild, Wild Women (Tower 1980)
6. Ace in the Hole (Tower 1981)
7. Yukon Ride (Tower 1981)

275. SAGA OF THE SOUTHWEST
By Leigh Franklin James
A saga about John Cooper Baines, alias The Hawk. The series was put together by Book Creations Inc.
1. The Hawk and the Dove (Bantam 1980)
2. Wings of the Hawk (Bantam 1981)
3. Revenge of the Hawk (Bantam 1981)
4. Flight of the Hawk (Bantam 1982)
5. Night of the Hawk (Bantam 1983)
6. Cry of the Hawk (Bantam 1984)
7. Quest of the Hawk (Bantam 1985)
8. Shadow of the Hawk (Bantam 1985)

276. SANTA FE TRAIL TRILOGY
By Harry Fergusson
The trio of books was also printed in a single volume.
   Wolf Song (Knopf 1927)
   In Those Days (Knopf 1929) (Corgi 1956)
   Blood of the Conquerors (Knopf 1931) (Chapman and Hall 1922)
   Followers of the Sun: A Trilogy of the Santa Fe Trail (Knopf 1936) Santa Fe Omnibus (Grosset and Dunlap 1938)

277. SAVAGE DESTINY
By F. Rosanne Bittner
This saga is about Abigail and Lone Eagle.
1. Sweet Prairie Passion (Zebra 1983)
2. Ride the Free Wind (Zebra 1984)
3. River of Love (Zebra 1984)
4. Embrace the Wild Land (Zebra 1984)
5. Climb the Highest Mountain (Zebra 1985)
6. Meet the New Dawn (Zebra 1986)

278. SAVAGE ROMANCES
By Constance O'Banyon
The books are about white woman Joanne's romance with the Indian Windhawk.
   Savage Desire (Zebra 1983)
   Savage Splendor (Zebra 1983)
   Savage Autumn (Zebra)
   Savage Winter (Zebra 1985)

279. TOM SAWYER
By Mark Twain
Samuel L. Clemens wrote these books about adventurous Missouri youth, marginally Westerns but of the proper period.
The Adventures of Tom Sawyer (1876)
The Adventures of Huckleberry Finn (1884)
Tom Sawyer Abroad (1894)
Tom Sawyer, Detective (1896)

280. SCARLET RIDERS
By Ian Anderson
Cavanaugh rides north to join the newly formed Northwest Mounted Police.
    1. Corporal Cavannaugh (McClelland & Stewart) (Zebra 1985)
    2. The Return of Cavanaugh (Zebra 1986)

281. THE SCOUT
By Buck Gentry
Eli Holten lived with the Sioux for six years and now is an Army scout in this adult series.
    1. Rowan's Raiders (Zebra 1981)
    2. Dakota Massace (Zebra 1981)
    3. Outlaw Canyon (Zebra 1981)
    4. Cheyenne Vengeance (Zebra 1982)
    5. Sioux Slaughter (Zebra 1982)
    6. Bandit Fury (Zebra 1982)
    7. Prairie Bush (Zebra 1982)
    8. Pawnee Rampage (Zebra 1983)
    9. Apache Ambush (Zebra 1983)
    10. Traitor's Gold (Zebra 1983)
    11. Yaqui Terror (Zebra 1983)
    12. Yellowstone Kill (Zebra 1983)
    13. Oglala Outbreak (Zebra 1983)
    14. Cathouse Canyon (Zebra 1984)
    15. Texas Tease (Zebra 1984)
    16. Virgin Outpost (Zebra 1985)
    17. Breakneck Bawdy House (Zebra 1985)
    18. Redskin Thrust (Zebra 1985)
    19. Big Top Squaw (Zebra 1985)

282. SHELTER
By Paul Ledd
Shelter Morgan is a revenge-seeking cowboy in this adult series.
    1. Prisoner of Revenge (Zebra 1980)
    2. Hanging Moon (Zebra 1980)
    3. Chain Gang Kill (Zebra 1980)
    4. China Doll (Zebra 1980)
    5. The Lazarus Guns (Zebra 1980)
    6. Circus of Death (Zebra 1981)

7. Lookout Mountain (Zebra 1981)
8. The Bandit Queen (Zebra 1981)
9. Apache Trail (Zebra 1982)
10. Massacre Mountain (Zebra 1982)
11. Rio Rampage (Zebra 1982)
12. Blood Mesa (Zebra 1983)
13. Comanchero Blood (Zebra 1983)
14. The Golden Shaft (Zebra 1983)
15. Savage Night (Zebra 1983)
16. Wichita Gunman (Zebra 1984)
17. The Naked Outpost (Zebra 1984)
18. Taboo Territory (Zebra 1984)
19. The Hard Men (Zebra 1984)
20. Saddle Tramp (Zebra 1984)
21. Shotgun Sugar (Zebra 1985)
22. Fast-Draw Filly (Zebra 1985)
23. Wanted Woman (Zebra 1985)

283. WILD HORSE SHORTY
By Nelson Nye
Shorty is a stubborn Westerner whose two novels were twice packaged in double volumes, by Ace and Zebra.
Wild Horse Shorty (Ace 1944)
Blood of Kings (Ace 1946)

284. SILVER CHIEF
By Jack O'Brien
The great grey dog and his master, Sgt. Jim Thorne of the RCMP, share juvenile adventures.
Silver Chief, Dog of the North (John C. Winston 1933) (Grosset & Dunlap)
Silver Chief to the Rescue (John C. Winston 1937) (Grosset & Dunlap)
The Return of Silver Chief (John C. Winston 1943) (Grosset & Dunlap)
Silver Chief's Revenge (John C. Winston 1954) (Grosset & Dunlap)

285. SILVERTIP
By Max Brand
Frederick Faust penned this series about Arizona Jim Silver. Entries have been issued in paper by Pocket, Warner and Paperback Library.
Silvertip (Dodd, Mead 1942) (Hodder and Stoughton 1942)
The Man from Mustang (Doddd, Mead 1942) (Hodder and Stoughton 1943)
Silvertip's Strike (Dodd, Mead 1942) (Hodder and Stoughton 1944)
Silvertip's Roundup (Dodd, Mead 1943) (Hodder and Stoughton 1945)
Silvertip's Trap (Dodd, Mead 1944) (Hodder and Stoughton 1946)
Silvertip's Chase (Blakiston 1944) (Hodder and Stoughton 1946)
Silvertip's Search (Dodd, Mead 1945) (Hodder and Stoughton 1948)
Stolen Stallion (Dodd, Mead 1945) (Hodder and Stoughton 1949)

286. JEREMY SIX
By Brian Wynne
Brian Garfield wrote these books about Marshal Jeremy Six of Spanish
Flat. The last entry features the town, but not the marshal. Running
characters include Dominguez, a deputy, and Clarissa Vane, a good
friend who is killed in *Big Country, Big Men.*
  Mr. Sixgun (Ace 1964)
  The Night It Rained Bullets (Ace 1965)
  The Bravos (Ace 1966)
  The Proud Riders (Ace 1967)
  A Badge for a Badman (Ace 1967)
  Brand of the Gun (Ace 1968)
  Gundown (Ace 1969)
  Big Country, Big Men (Ace 1969)
  Justice at Spanish Flat (Ace)

287. SIX-GUN SAMURAI
By Patrick Lee
Tanaka Tom Fletcher, an American, was raised in the land of the
Shogun in Japan and trained as a warrior. He abides by the Samurai
code of Bushido. He is on a bloody vendetta against the killers of his
family. Various entries are copyright W.L. Fieldhouse and Mark K.
Roberts. The series, initially called Six-Gun Samurai, became Six-Gun
Warrior with the seventh entry.
  1. Six-Gun Samurai (Pinnacle 1981)
  2. Bushido Vengeance (Pinnacle 1981)
  3. Gundown at Golden Gate (Pinncale 1981)
  4. Kamakazi Justice (Pinnacle 1981)
  5. The Devil's Bowman (Pinnacle 1981)
  6. Bushido Lawman (Pinnacle 1982)
  7. Prairie Caesar (Pinnacle 1982)
  8. Apache Messiah (?) (Pinnacle 1983)

SIX-GUN WARRIOR
See SIX-GUN SAMURAI

288. WALT SLADE
By Bradford Scott
Slade, the undercover ace of the Texas Rangers, appeared in the *Thrill-
ing Western* pulp and made a transition to original paperbacks. A. Leslie
Scott wrote the series.
  Canyon Killers (Pyramid 1956)
  Border Blood (Pyramid 1956)
  The Texas Terror (Pyramid 1956)
  Trigger Talk (Pyramid 1956)
  Badlands Boss (Pyramid 1956)
  Death Canyon (Pyramid 1957)
  Dead Man's Trail (Pyramid 1957)

Powder Burn (Pyramid 1957)
Curse of Texas Gold (Pyramid 1957)
The Texas Hawk (Pyramid 1957)
Shootin' Man (Pyramid 1958)
The Blaze of Guns (Pyramid 1958)
Dead in Texas (Pyramid 1959)
Texas Badman (Pyramid 1959)
Texas Vengeance (Pyramid 1959)
The Range Terror (Pyramid 1959)
Gun Law (Pyramid 1959)
Holster Law (Pyramid 1959)
Valley of Hunted Man (Pyramid 1960)
Ambush Trail (Pyramid 1960)
Gun Gamble (Pyramid 1960)
The Pecos Trail (Pyramid 1960)
Lone Star Rider (Pyramid 1960)
Guns of the Alamo (Pyramid 1960)
Desert Killers (Pyramid 1961)
Rangeland Guns (Pyramid 1961)
Rangers at Bay (Pyramid 1961)
Skeleton Trail (Pyramid 1961)
Smuggler's Brand (Pyramid 1961)
Gunsmoke on the Rio Grande (Pyramid 1961)
Masked Riders (Pyramid 1962)
Texas Rider (Pyramid 1962)
Gunsight Showdown (Pyramid 1962)
Doom Trail (Pyramid 1962)
A Ranger Rides to Death (Pyramid 1962)
Guns of Bang Town (Pyramid 1962)
Texas Devil (Pyramid 1962)
Death Rides the Rio Grande (Pyramid 1962)
Rustler's Range (Pyramid 1963)
Gundown (Pyramid 1963)
Ranger's Revenge (Pyramid 1963)
Rattlesnake Bandit (Pyramid 1963)
Rustler's Guns (Pyramid 1963)
Hate Trail (Pyramid 1963)
Gunsmoke Talk (Pyramid 1963)
Death's Corral (Pyramid 1963)
Outlaw Land (Pyramid 1963)
Killer's Doom (Pyramid 1963)
Bullets for a Ranger (Pyramid 1963)
Outlaw's Gold (Pyramid 1963)
Raiders of the Rio Grande (Pyramid 1964)
Guns For Hire (Pyramid 1964)
Dead at Sunset (Pyramid 1964)
Tombstone Showdown (Pyramid 1964)
Bullet Brand (Pyramid 1966)

Maverick Showdown (Pyramid 1967)
Hot Lead and Cold Nerve (Pyramid 1967)
Death's Tally (Pyramid 1968)
Hard Rock Showdown (Pyramid 1968)
The River Raiders (Pyramid 1968)
Curse of Dead Man's Gold (Pyramid 1969)
Trail of Empire (Pyramid 1969)
Devil from Blazing Hill (A Ranger to the Rescue) (Pyramid 1969)
Hands Up (Pyramid 1969)
Rider of the Mesquite Trail (Pyramid 1969)
Sixgun Doom (Pyramid 1969)
Sixgun Talk (Trigger Talk) (Pyramid 1969)
Texas Blood (Blood and Steel) (Pyramid 1969
Trail of Empire (Pyramid 1969)
Sidewinder (Pyramid 1969)
Death Whisper (Pyramid 1970)
Ranger's Roundup (Follow the Ranger Roundup) (Pyramid 1970)
Reach for Gold (Pyramid 1970)
Death to the Ranger (Pyramid 1970)
Savage Gunlaw (Pyramid 1971)
Ranger Wins (Pyramid 1971)
Stranger in Boots (Pyramid 1971)
Ranger Daring (Pyramid 1971)
Border Terror (Pyramid 1972)
Spargo (Pyramid 1972)
Border Daring (Pyramid 1973)
Death's Harvest (Pyramid 1973)
Four Must Die (Pyramid 1973)
The Ranger Rides the Death Trail (Pyramid)
Canyon Killers (Pyramid)
Gunsmoke Over Texas (Pyramid)
The Avenger (Pyramid)
Dead Man's Trail (Pyramid)
Rimrock Raiders (Pyramid)

289. TORN SLATER
By Jackson Cain
Slater is an outlaw in this adult series which features historical characters such as Calamity Jane and Wild Bill Hickok. The author is Robert Gleason.
1. Hellbreak Country (Warner 1984)
2. Savage Blood (Warner 1984)
3. Hangman's Whip (Warner 1984)
4. Hell Hound (Warner 1984)
5. Devil's Sting (Warner 1985)

290. SLATTERY
By Steven C. Lawrence
This series about Tom Slattery was originally published by Ace in double volumes. Leisure re-issued the series in single volumes.
Slattery/Bullet Welcome for Slattery (Ace 1961) 1. The Lynchers (Leisure 1975) 2. Bullet Welcome (Leisure 1975)
A Noose for Slattery/Walk a Narrow Trail (Ace 1962) 3. A Noose for Slattery (Leisure 1975) 4. Walk a Narrow Trail (Leisure 1975)
Slattery's Gun Says No/Longhorns North (Ace 1962) 5. Slattery's Gun Says No (Leisure 1975) 6. North to Montana (Leisure 1975)
7. Slattery Stands Alone (Leisure 1976)
8. Day of the Comancheros (Leisure 1977)

291. JOHN SLAUGHTER
By Various Authors
The historical character was featured in unrelated offerings. The third listing was reprinted in paperback by Curtis.
Slaughter's Way by J.T. Edson (Brown Watson 1965)
Slaughter's Neighbors (Corgi announced)
John Slaughter's Way by James Wyckoff (Doubleday 1963)

292. SLAUGHTER & SON
By E.B. Majors
The series is about veteran field detective Bert Slaughter and his college-educated son Ben.
1. Slaughter & Son (Warner 1985)
2. Nightmare Trail (Warner 1985)
3. Hair Trigger Kill (Warner 1985)

293. SLOANE
By Steve Lee
Sloane is a martial arts cowboy.
1. The Man with the Iron Fists (Futura 1974) (Pinnacle 1974)
2. A Fistful of Hate (Future 1975) (Pinnacle 1975)

294. SLOCUM
By Jake Logan
Slocum is an adult Western series written under a house name. It was picked up by Berkley after Playboy's demise, apparently skipping some numbers.
1. Ride, Slocum, Ride (by Howard Pehrson) (Playboy 1975)
2. Hanging Justice (by Jack M. Bickham) (Playboy 1975)
3. Slocum and the Widow Kate (Playboy 1975)
4. Across the Rio Grande (Playboy 1975)
5. The Comanche's Woman (Playboy 1975)
6. Slocum's Gold (by Pehrson) (Playboy 1976)
7. Bloody Trail to Texas (Playboy 1976)
8. North to Dakota (by Martin Cruz Smith) (Playboy 1976)

9. Slocum's Woman (Playboy 1977)
10. White Hell (Playboy 1977)
11. Ride for Revenge (by Smith) (Playboy)
12. Outlaw Blood (Playboy)
13. Montana Showdown (Playboy)
14. See Texas and Die (Playboy);
15. Iron Mustang (Playboy 1978)
16. Slocum's Blood (Playboy)
17. Slocum's Fire (Playboy)
18. Slocum's Revenge (Playboy)
19. Slocum's Hell (Playboy)
20. Slocum's Grave (Playboy)
21. Shotguns from Hell (Playboy)
22. Dead Man's Hand (Playboy 1979)
23. Fighting Vengeance (Playboy 1980)
24. Slocum's Slaughter (Playboy 1980)
25. Roughrider (Playboy 1980)
26. Slocum's Rage (Playboy 1981)
27. Hellfire (Playboy 1981)
28. Slocum's Code (Playboy 1981)
29. Slocum's Raid (Playboy 1981)
30. Slocum's Flag (Playboy 1981)
31. Slocum's Run (Playboy 1981)
32. Slocum's Gamble (Playboy 1982)
33. Slocum's Debt (Playboy 1982)
34. Slocum and the Mad Major (Playboy 1982)
35. The Necktie Party (Playboy 1982)
36. The Canyon Bunch (Playboy 1982)
37. Blazing Guns (Playboy 1982)
38. Swamp Foxes (Playboy 1982)
39. Law Comes to Cold Rain (Playboy 1982)
40. Slocum's Pride (Playboy 1982)
50. Slocum's Drive (Berkley 1983)
51. Jackson Hole Trouble (Berkley 1983)
52. Silver City Shootout (Berkley 1983)
53. Slocum and the Law (Berkley 1983)
54. Apache Sunrise (Berkley 1983)
55. Slocum's Justice (Berkley 1983)
56. Nebraska Burnout (Berkley 1983)
57. Slocum and the Cattle Queen (Berkley 1983)
58. Slocum's Women (Berkley 1983)
59. Slocum's Command (Berkley 1983)
60. Slocum Gets Even (Berkley 1983)
61. Slocum and the Lost Dutchman Mine (Berkley 1984)
62. High Country Holdup (Berkley 1984)
63. Guns of South Pass (Berkley 1984)
64. Slocum and the Hatchet Men (Berkley 1984)
65. Bandit Gold (Berkley 1984)

66. South of the Border (Berkley 1984)
67. Dallas Madam (Berkley 1984)
68. Texas Showdown (Berkley 1984)
69. Slocum in Deadwood (Berkley 1984)
70. Slocum's Winning Hand (Berkley 1984)
71. Slocum and the Gun Runners (Berkley 1984)
72. Across the Rio Grande (Berkley 1984)
73. Slocum's Crime (Berkley 1984)
74. Nevada Swindle (Berkley 1985)
75. Slocum's Good Deed (Berkley 1985)
76. Slocum's Stampede (Berkley 1985)
77. Gunplay at Hobb's Hole (Berkley 1985)
78. The Journey of Death (Berkley 1985)
79. Slocum and the Avenging Gun (Berkley 1985)
80. Slocum Rides Alone (Berkley 1985)
81. The Sunshine Basin War (Berkley 1985)
82. Vigilante Justice (Berkley 1985)
83. Jailbreak Moon (Berkley 1985)
84. Six-Gun Bride (Berkley 1985)
85. Mescalero Dawn (Berkley 1985)
86. Denver Gold (Berkley 1986)
87. Slocum and the Bozeman Trail (Berkley 1986)
88. Slocum and the Horse Theives (Berkley 1986)
89. Slocum and the Noose of Hell (Berkley 1986)

295. WAXAHACHIE SMITH
By J.T. Edson
This series is by the prolific British writer.
  No Finger on the Trigger (Corgi)
  Slip Gun (Corgi 1971)
  Waxahachie Smith (Corgi)
  Cure the Texas Fever (Corgi)

296. SAD SONTAG
By W.C. Tuttle
Singing River originally appeared in *West Magazine.*
  Sad Sontag Plays His Hunch (Garden City 1926)
  Sontag of Sundown (Garden City) (World's Work 1929)
  Singing River (Collins 1931) (Houghton Mifflin 1939)

297. SPANISH BIT SAGA
By Don Goldsmith
This hardcover series is about 16th century Plains Indians.
  Trail of the Spanish Bit (Doubleday)
  Buffalo Medicine (Doubleday)
  The Elk Dog Heritage (Doubleday)
  Follow the Wind (Doubleday)
  Man of the Shadows (Doubleday)

Daughter of the Eagle (Doubleday)
Moon of Thunder (Doubleday 1985)
The Sacred Hills (Doubleday 1985)
Pale Star (Doubleday 1986)

298. AGENT BRAD SPEAR
By Chet Cunningham and Chad Calhoun
The hero is a Pinkerton agent in this adult series under the Banbury imprint.
1. The Cheyenne Payoff by Chet Cunningham (Dell 1981)
2. The Silver Mistress by Cunningham (Dell 1981)
3. The Tucson Temptress by Cunningham (Dell 1981)
4. The Frisco Lady by Cunningham (Dell 1981)
5. The Painted Women by Cunningham (Greg Hunt) (Dell 1981)
6. The Hidden Princess by Chad Calhoun (Ron Goulart) (Dell 1982)
7.
8.
9. The Wild Dancer by Calhoun (Goulart) (Dell 1982)
10. The Lady Rustler by Calhoun (Goulart) (Dell 1982)
11.
12. The Gambler's Woman by Calhoun (Lee Hays) (Dell 1982)

299. SPECTROS
By Logan Winters
Dr. Spectros is a master magician in the Old West. The series was published by Manor and Tower.
1. Silverado (Tower 1981)
2. Hunt the Beast Down (Tower 1981)
3. Natchez (Tower 1981)
4. The Silver Galleon (Tower 1981)
Showdown at Guyamos (re-title?) (Manor 1978)

300. SPIRIT OF AMERICA
By Charles Whited
This saga is about the Stewart empire. The entries are Arthur Pines Associates books.
1. Challenge (Bantam 1982)
2. Destiny (Bantam 1982)

301. SPUR (I)
By Dirk Fletcher
Spur McCoy is an Easterner, a member of the government's Secret Service Agency, now serving in the West. This is an adult series.
1. High Plains Temptress (Leisure 1982)
2. Arizona Fancy Lady (Leisure 1982)
3. St. Louis Jezebel (Leisure 1982)
4. Rocky Mountain Vamp (Leisure 1982)
5. Wyoming Wench (Leisure 1984)
6. Texas Tart (Leisure 1984)

7. San Francisco Strumpet (Leisure 1984)
8. Montana Minx (Leisure 1984)
9. Cathouse Kitten (Leisure 1984)
10. Indian Maid (Leisure 1984)
11. Nebraska Nymph (Leisure 1985)
12. Gold Train Tramp (Leisure 1985)
13. Red Rock Redhead (Leisure 1985)
14. Savage Sisters (Leisure 1986)

302. SPUR (II)
By Cy James
The byline is a penname for British writer Peter Christopher Watts.
 The Cimarron Kid (Mayflower 1969)
 Trail West (Mayflower 1970)
 Longhorn (Mayflower 1970)
 Gun (Mayflower 1971)
 The Brave Ride Tall (Mayflower 1971)
 Blood at Sunset (Mayflower 1971)

303. STAGECOACH STATION
By Hank Mitchum
This series features a stagecoach station in a different city in each title. It
was put together by Book Creations Inc.
1. Dodge City (Bantam)
2. Laredo (Bantam)
3. Cheyenne (Bantam)
4. Tombstone (Bantam)
5. Virginia City (Bantam)
6. Santa Fe (Bantam)
7. Seattle (Bantam)
8. Fort Yuma (Bantam)
9. Sonora (Bantam)
10. Abilene (Bantam)
11. Deadwood (Bantam)
12. Tucson (Bantam)
13. Carson City (Bantam)
14. Cimarron (Bantam 1984)
15. Wichita (Bantam 1984)
16. Mojave (Bantam 1985)
17. Durango (Bantam 1985)
18. Casa Grande (Bantam 1985)
19. Last Chance (Bantam 1985)
20. Leadville (Bantam 1985)
21. Fargo (Bantam 1985)
22. Devil's Canyon (Bantam 1986)

304. STANTON SAGA
By Tom W. Blackburn

This series has been issued in two editions by the publisher.
1. Yanqui (Dell 1973)
2. Ranchero (Dell 1974)
3. El Segundo (Dell 1978)
4. Patron (Dell)
5. Companeros (Dell)

305. LUKE STARBUCK
By Matt Braun
There is a great deal of historical detail in this series.
1. Hangman's Creek (Pocket 1979) (Sphere 1982)
2. Jury of Six (Pocket 1980) (Sphere 1982)
3. Tombstone (Pocket 1981) (Sphere 1982)
4. The Spoilers (Pocket 1981) (Sphere 1982)
5. The Manhunter (Pocket 1981) (Sphere 1982)
6. Deadwood (Pocket 1981) (Sphere 1982)
7. The Judas Tree (Pocket 1982) (Sphere 1983)

306. SHAWN STARBUCK
By Ray Hogan
Starbuck is usually on the run from the law. Some of the books were issued as doubles by Signet.
1. The Rimrocker (Signet 1970)
2. The Outlawed (Signet 1970)
3. Three Cross (Signet 1970)
4. Deputy of Violence (Signet 1971)
5. A Bullet for Mr. Texas (Signet 1971)
6. Marshal of Babylon (Signet 1971)
7. Brandon's Posse (Signet 1971)
8. The Devil's Gunhand (Signet 1972)
9. Passage to Dodge City (Signet 1972)
10. The Hell Merchant (Signet 1972)
11. Lawman for the Slaughter (Signet 1972)
12. The Guns of Stingaree (Signet 1973)
13. Skull Gold (Signet 1973)
14. Highroller's Man (Signet 1973)
15. The Texas Brigade (Signet 1974)
16. The Jenner Guns (Signet 1974)
17. The Scorpion Killers (Signet 1974)
18. The Tombstone Trail (Signet 1974)
19. The Day of the Hangman (Signet 1975)
20. The Last Comanchero (Signet 1975)
21. High Green Gun (Signet 1976)
22. The Shotgun Rider (Signet 1976)
23. Bounty Hunter's Moon (Signet 197)
24. A Gun for Silver Rose (Signet 1977)

307. JIM STEEL
By Chet Cunningham
This series, about the Gold Man, has had three publishers: Pinnacle, Belmont Tower and Tower. Listed is the last edition.
1. Gold Wagon (Tower 1980)
2. Die of Gold (Tower 1980)
3. Bloody Gold (Tower 1980)
4. Devil's Gold (Tower 1980)
5. Gold Train (Tower 1981)
6. Axtec Gold (Tower 1981)

308. STEELE
By George G. Gilman
Terry Harknett penned this series, a violent one about Virginian Adam Steele in the West. The books were originally published in England. See also Edge Meets Steele entry.
1. The Violent Peace (New English Library 1974) Rebels and Assassins Die Hard (Pinnacle 1975)
2. The Bounty Hunter (New English Library 1974) (Pinnacle 1975)
3. Hell's Junction (New English Library 1974) (Pinnacle 1976)
4. Valley of Blood (New English Library 1975) (Pinnacle 1976)
5. Gun Run (New English Library 1975) (Pinnacle 1976)
6. The Killing Art (New English Library 1975) (Pinnacle 1976)
7. Cross-Fire (New English Library 1975) (Pinnacle 1976)
8. Comanche Carnage (New English Library 1976) (Pinnacle 1977)
9. Badge in the Dust (New English Library 1976) (Pinnacle 1977)
10. The Losers (New English Library 1976) (Pinnacle 1978)
11. Lynch Town (New English Library 1976) (Pinnacle 1978)
12. Death Trail (New English Library 1977) (Pinnacle 1978)
13. Bloody Border (New English Library 1977) (Pinnacle 1979)
14. Delta Duel (New English Library 1977) (Pinnacle 1979)
15. River of Death (New English Library 1977) (Pinnacle 1980)
16. Nightmare at Noon (New English Library 197) (Pinnacle 1980)
17. Satan's Daughters (New English Library 1978) (Pinnacle 1980)
18. The Hard Way (New English Library 1978) (Pinnacle 1980)
19. The Tarnished Star (New English Library 1979) (Pinnacle 1981)
20. Wanted for Murder (New English Library 1979) (Pinnacle 1982)
21. Wagons East (New English Library 1979) (Pinnacle 1082)
22. The Big Game (New English Library 1979) (Pinnacle 1982)
23. Fort Despair (New English Library 1979) (Pinnacle 1983)
24. Manhunt (New English Library 1980) (Pinnacle 1983)
25. The Woman (New English Library 1980) Steele's War: The Women (Pinnacle 1984)
26. The Preacher (New English Library 1981) Steele's War: The Preacher (Pinnacle 1984)
27. The Storekeeper (New English Library 1981)
28. The Stranger (New English Library 1981)

29. The Big Prize (New English Library 1981)
30. The Killer Mountains (New English Library 1982)
31. The Cheaters (New English Library 1982)

309. SHERIFF BLUE STEELE
By Tom Gunn
Entries in this series appeared in hardcover and pulp formats. One entry
is copyright by Syl MacDowell. Steele is the law in Painted Post.
The Sheriff of Painted Post (Pocket 1951)
Painted Post Law (Pocket 1952)
Painted Post Range (Pocket 1953)
Painted Post Gunplay (Pocket 1954)
Painted Post Outlaws (Harlequin)

310. STORM
By Matt Chisholm
The author is English writer Peter Christopher Watts.
Stampede (Panther 1970)
Hard Texas Trail (Panther 1971)
Riders West (Mayflower 1971)
One Notch to Death (Mayflower 1972)
One Man — One Gun (Mayflower 1972)
Thunder in the West (Mayflower 1972)
A Breed of Men (Mayflower 1973)
Battle Fury (Mayflower 1973)
Blood on the Hills (Mayflower 1973)

311. THE STORY OF CALIFORNIA
By Stewart Edward White
The three novels were collected in the fourth entry.
Gold (Doubleday 1913) (Hodder & Stoughton 1914)
The Gray Dawn (Doubleday 1915) (Hodder & Stoughton 1915)
The Rose Dawn (Doubleday 1920) (Hodder & Stoughton 1921)
The Story of California (Doubleday 1927)

312. THE STORY OF CANADA
By Dennis Adair and Janet Rosenstock
This saga is about the MacLeods in Canada
1. Kanata (Avon 1981)
2. Bitter Shield (Avon 1982)
3. Thundergate (Avon 1982)
4. Wildfires (Avon 1983)
5. Victoria (Avon 1983)

313. SUDDEN
By Oliver Strange and Frederick H. Christian
Sudden is a hard-nosed gunfighter.

Sudden — Outlawed by Oliver Strange
Sudden by Strange
The Marshal of Lawless by Strange
Sudden — Goldseeker by Strange
Sudden Rides Again by Strange
Sudden Takes the Trail by Strange
The Range Robbers by Strange
Sudden Plays A Hand by Strange
Sudden Strikes Back by Frederick H. Christian (Corgi 1966)
Sudden — Troubleshooter by Christian (Corgi 1967)
Sudden At Bay by Christian (Corgi 1968)
Sudden — Apache Fighter by Christian (Corgi 1969)
Sudden — Dead or Alive! by Christian (Corgi 1970)

314. SUNDANCE
By Various Authors
Jim Sundance is part English, part Cheyenne in this violent series.
1. Overkill by John Benteen (by Ben Haas) (Leisure 1974)
2. Dead Man's Canyon by Benteen (by Haas) (Leisure 1974)
3. Dakota Territory by Benteen (Leisure 1974)
4. Death in the Lava by Benteen (by Haas) (Leisure 1974)
5. The Pistoleros by Benteen (by Haas) (Leisure 1974)
6. The Bronco Trail by Benteen (by Haas) (Leisure 1974)
7. The Wild Stallions by Benteen (by Haas) (Leisure)
8. Bring Me His Scalp by Benteen (Leisure 1973)
9. Taps at Little Big Horn by Benteen (by Haas) (Leisure 1974)
10. The Ghost Dancers by Benteen (by Haas) (Leisure 1974)
11. The Comancheros by Benteen (Leisure 1974)
12. Renegade by Benteen (Leisure 1974)
13. Honcho by Jack Slade (Leisure)
14. War Party by Slade (Leisure)
15. Bounty Killer by Slade (Leisure)
16. Run for Cover by Slade (Haas) (Leisure)
17. Manhunt by Slade (Haas) (Leisure)
18. Blood on the Prairie by Slade (Leisure)
19. War Trail by Slade (Leisure)
20. Riding Shotgun by Slade (Haas) (Leisure)
21. Silent Enemy by Slade (Haas) (Leisure)
22. Ride the Man Down by Slade (Leisure)
23. Gunbelt by Slade (Leisure)
24. Canyon Kill by Slade (Leisure 1979)
25. Blood Knife by Slade (Leisure 1979)
26. Nightriders by Peter McCurtin (Leisure 1979)
27. Death Dance by McCurtin (Leisure 1979)
28. The Savage by McCurtin (Leisure 1979)
29. Day of the Halfbreeds by McCurtin (Leisure 1979)
30. Los Olvidados by McCurtin (Leisure 1979)
31. The Marauders by McCurtin (Leisure 1980)

32. Scorpion by McCurtin (Leisure 1980)
33. Hangman's Knot by McCurtin (Leisure 1980)
34. Apache War by McCurtin (Leisure 1980)
35. Gold Strike by McCurtin (Leisure 1980)
36. Trail Drive by McCurtin (Leisure 1981)
37. Iron Men by McCurtin (Leisure 1981)
38. Drumfire by McCurtin (Leisure 1982)
39. Buffalo War by McCurtin (Leisure 1982)
40. The Hunters by McCurtin (Leisure 1981)
41. The Cage by McCurtin (Leisure 1982)
42. Choctaw County War by McCurtin (Leisure 1982)
43. Texas Empire by McCurtin (Leisure 1982)

315. SUSANNAH OF THE YUKON
By Muriel Denison
The stories are about a young girl in the north.
Susannah, A Little Girl with the Mounties (Dodd, Mead)
Susannah of the Yukon (Dodd, Mead 1938)
Susannah at Boarding School (Dodd, Mead 1938)

316. LUKE SUTTON
By Leo P. Kelley
Sutton is seeking the outlaws who killed his brother. The series was
reprinted in paper by Signet.
Luke Sutton: Outlaw (Doubleday 1981)
Luke Sutton: Gunfighter (Doubleday 1982)
Luke Sutton: Indian Fighter (Doubleday 1982)
Luke Sutton: Avenger (Doubleday 1984)
Luke Sutton: Outrider (Doubleday 1984)
Luke Sutton: Bounty Hunter (Doubleday 1985)

317. SWEET MEDICINE'S PROPHECY
By Karen A. Bale
This is an Indian romance saga series.
1. Sundancer's Passion (Zebra)
2. Little Flower's Desire (Zebra)
3. Winter's Love (Zebra)
4. Savage Fury (Zebra 1986)

318. TAIL END RANCH
By John H. Culp
The Kid and the daredevil crew of the Tail End Ranch are featured in
these titles, which also appeared in hardcover.
Born of the Sun (Ace)
The Restless Land (Ace)

319. TALES OF A MINNESOTA GIRL
By Frances R. Sterrett

This is a girls' book series.
  Rusty of the Tall Pines (Penn 1928)
  Rusty of the High Towers (Penn 1929)
  Rusty of the Mountain Peaks (Penn 1930)
  Rusty of the Meadow Lands (Penn 1931)

320. TALES OF TEXAS
  By Elmer Kelton
Bantam repackaged the books by the Lone Star State-born author under
this banner.
  Horsehead Crossing (Ballantine 1963)
  Massacre at Goliad (Ballantine 1965) (New English Library 1967)
  Llano River (Ballantine 1966) (Panther 1968)
  After the Bugles (Ballantine 1967)
  Hanging Judge (Ballantine 1969)
  Captain's Rangers (Ballantine 1969) (Arrow 1971)
  Bowie's Mine (Ballantine 1971)
  Wagontongue (as by Lee McElroy) (Ballantine 1972)
  Manhunt (Ballantine 1974)
  The Wolf and the Buffalo (Doubleday 1980)
  Eyes of the Hawk (as by McElroy) (Doubleday 1981)
  Stand Proud (Doubleday 1984)

321. TALES OF WELLS FARGO
  By Various Authors
Frank Gruber, one of the creative forces behind the televison program
"Tales of Wells Fargo" (1957-62), wrote the short stories collected in the
first volume listed below.
  Tales of Wells Fargo by Frank Gruber (Bantam 1958)
  Tales of Wells Fargo: Danger at Dry Creek (Golden Press)
  Wells Fargo: Danger Station by Noel Loomis (Whitman 1958)

322. THE TALL MAN
  By Clay Fisher
Ben Allison is a rangy Westerner in this series penned by Henry Wilson
Allen.
  The Tall Men (Houghton Mifflin 1954) (World's Work 1956)
  The Crossing (Houghton Mifflin 1958) River of Decision (Corgi 1958)
  Return of the Tall Man (Pocket 1961)
  Outcasts of Canyon Creek (Bantam 1972)
  Apache Ransom (Bantam 1974)

323. ASH TALLMAN
  By Tom Lord
Tallman is a Pinkerton cop in this adult series.
  1. The Highbinders (Avon 1983)
  2. Crossfire (Avon 1984)
  3. The Wages of Sin (Avon 1984)

324. THE TEXAN
   By Joseph A. Altsheler
These are boys' book stories of the Texas war for independence.
   The Texan Star (D. Appleton 1912)
   The Texan Scouts (D. Appleton 1913)
   The Texan Triumph (D. Appleton 1913)

TEXAS LAWMAN
   See FLAGG

TEXAS RANGERS
   See HATFIELD

325. THE TEXIANS
   By Zach Wyatt
The series features Capt. Jack Hayes, Josh Sands and other members of
the Texas Rangers. The stories are copyright by George W. Proctor.
   1. The Texians (Pinnacle 1984)
   2. Horse Marines (Pinnacle 1984)
   3. War Devils (Pinnacle 1984)
   4. Blood Moon (Pinnacle 1985)
   5. Death's Shadow (Pinnacle 1985)

326. CALEB THORN
   By L.J. Coburn
John G. Harvey wrote some entries in this series.
   1.
   2. The Raiders by John G. Harvey) (Sphere 1977)
   3.
   4. Bloody Shiloh (by Harvey) (Sphere 1978)

327. TOMMY THORNE
   By Charles H. Snow
This was a British series.
   The Lakeside Murder (Wright and Brown 1933)
   The Bonanza Murder Case (Wright and Brown 1934)
   The Sign of the Death Circle (Wright and Brown 1935)

328. THREE BOYS SERIES
   By Egerton Ryerson Young
This is a boys' book series.
   Three Boys in the Wild North Land (Eaton and Mains 1896)
   Winter Adventures of Three Boys in Great Lone Land (Eaton and
Mains 1899)

329. THE THREE MESQUITEERS
   By William Colt MacDonald
Tucson Smith, Lullaby Joslin and Stony Brooke — the Three Mes-
quiteers — were featured in pulp stories in the 1930s and in a series of

B-Western movies. Paperback reprints were issued by Avon and Gunfire Western Novel.
Law of the Forty-Fives (Covici Friede 1933) (Collins 1934) The Sunrise Guns (Avon 1960)
The Singing Scorpion (Covici Friede 1934) (Collins 1935) Ambush at Scorpion Valley (Avon 1963)
Powdersmoke Range (Covici Friede 1934) (Collins 1935)
Riders of the Whistling Skull (Covici Friede 1934) (Collins 1935)
Roarin' Lead (Covici Friede 1935) (Collins 1936)
Rebel Ranger (Doubleday 1943) (Hodder and Stoughton 1945)
The Vanishing Gunslinger (Doubleday 1943)
The Three Mesquiteers (Doubleday 1944)
Thunderbird Trail (Doubleday 1946)
Bad Man's Return: A Three Mesquiteers Story (Doubleday 1947) (Hodder and Stoughton 1950)
Powdersmoke Justice (Doubleday 1949) (Hodder and Stoughton 1951)
Mesquiteer Mavericks (Doubleday 1950) (Hodder and Stoughton 1951)
The Galloping Ghost (Doubleday 1952) (Hodder and Stoughton 1955)

330. THREE RIVERS
By James Oliver Curwood
The Royal Canadian Mounted Police figure in this series.
The River's End (Cosmopolitan 1919)
The Valley of Silent Men (Cosmopolitan 1920)
The Flaming Forest (Cosmopolitan 1921)

331. THUNDER MOON
By Max Brand
Frederick Faust wrote this series of pulp novelettes as Max Brand. They are about a Cheyenne warrior and were reprinted in paperback by Warner.
Thunder Moon's Challenge (Dodd, Mead 1983)
Thunder Moon's Strike (Dodd, Mead 1984)

332. TOWN TAMER
By Barry Cord
Luke Ryatt has the nickname Town Tamer. The book carries the blurb "A Town Tamer Western." There may be others in the series.
Dodge City (Manor 1976)

333. TRACKER
By Tom Cutter
Tracker owns one of the fanciest hotels in San Francisco in this adult series by Robert J. Randisi.
1. The Winning Hand (Avon 1983)
2. Lincoln County (Avon 1983)
3. The Blue Cut Jib (Avon 1983)
4. Chinatown Chance (Avon 1983)

  5. Oklahoma Score (Avon 1985)
  6. Barbary Coast Tong (Avon 1985)
  7. Huntsville Breakout (Avon 1985)

334. TRAIL BLAZERS
By Various Authors
This is a boys' book series later called the American Trail Blazers Series.
Capt. John Smith by H.C. Forbes-Lindsey (J.B. Lippincott 1907)
Daniel Boone, Backwoodsman by Forbes-Lindsey (J.B. Lippincott 1908)
David Crockett, Scout by Charles Fletcher Allen (J.B. Lippincott 1911)
With Carson and Fremont by Edward L. Sabin (J.B. Lippincott 1912)
On the Plains with Custer by Sabin (J.B. Lippincott 1913)
Buffalo Bill and the Overland Trail by Sabin (J.B. Lippincott 1914)
Gold Seeker of '49 by Sabin (J.B. Lippincott 1915)
With Sam Houston in Texas by Sabin (J.B. Lippincott 1916)
Opening the West with Lewis and Clark by Sabin (J.B. Lippincott 1917)
General Crook and the Fighting Apaches (J.B. Lippincott 1918)
Lost with Lieutenant Pike by Sabin (J.B. Lippincott 1919)
Into Mexico with General Scott by Sabin (J.B. Lippincott 1920)
With George Washington Into the West by Sabin (J.B. Lippincott 1924)
In the Ranks of Old Hickory by Sabin (J.B. Lippincott 1927)
Mississippi River Boy by Sabin (J.B. Lippincott 1932)

335. THE TRAILSMAN
By Jon Sharpe
Skye Fargo is a scout and hunter in this adult series.
  1. Seven Wagons West (Signet 1980)
  2. The Hanging Trail (Signet 1980)
  3. Mountain Man Kill (Signet 1980)
  4. The Sundown Searchers (Signet 1980)
  5. The River Raiders (Signet 1981)
  6. Dakota Wild (Signet 1981)
  7. Wolf Country (Signet 1981)
  8. Six-Gun Drive (Signet 1981)
  9. Dead Man's Saddle (Signet 1982)
  10. Slave Hunter (Signet 1982)
  11. Montana Maiden (Signet 1982)
  12. Condor Pass (Signet 1982)
  13. Blood Chase (Signet 1982)
  14. Arrowhead Territory (Signet 1983)
  15. The Stalking Horse (Signet 1983)
  16. Savage Showdown (Signet 1983)
  17. Ride the Wild Shadows (Signet 1983)
  18. Cry the Cheyenne (Signet 1983)
  19. Spoon River Stud (Signet 1983)
  20. The Judas Killer (Signet 1983)
  21. Whisky Guns (Signet 1983)

22. Border Arrows (Signet 1983)
23. The Comstock Killers (Signet 1983)
24. Twisted Noose (Signet 1983)
25. Maverick Maiden (Signet 1984)
26. Warpaint and Rifles (Signet 1984)
27. Bloody Heritage (Signet 1984)
28. Hostage Trail (Signet 1984)
29. High Mountain Guns (Signet 1984)
30. White Savage (Signet 1984)
31. Six-Gun Sombreros (Signet 1984)
32. Apache Gold (Sigent 1984)
33. Red River Revenge (Signet 1984)
34. Sharps Justice (Signet 1984)
35. Kiowa Kill (Signet 1984)
36. The Badge (Signet 1984)
37. Valley of Death (Signet 1985)
38. Tomahawk Revenge (Signet 1985)
39. Grizzley Man (Signet 1985)
40. The Lost Patrol (Signet 1985)
41. The Range Killers (Signet 1985)
42. Renegade Command (Signet 1985)
43. Mesquite Manhunt (Signet 1985)
44. Scorpion Trail (Signet 1985)
45. Killer Caravan (Signet 1985)
46. Hell Town (Signet 1985)
47. Six-Gun Salvation (Signet 1985)
48. The White Hell Trail (Signet 1985)
49. Swamp Slayer (Signet 1986)
50. Blood Oath (Signet 1986)
51. Sioux Captive (Signet 1986)
52. Posse from Hell (Signet 1986)
53. Longhorn Guns (Signet 1986)

336. DOC TRAVIS
By Lou Cameron
The books blend humor and action.
Doc Travis (Dell 1975)
North to Cheyenne (Dell 1975)
The Guns of Durango (Dell 1976)

337. THE UNDERTAKER
By George G. Gilman
Barnaby Gold, son of a Texas undertaker, becomes a vengeance-seeking killer in this Terry Harknett series from England.
1. Black as Death (New English Library 1981) (Pinnacle 1985)
2. Destined to Die (New English Library 1981) (Pinnacle 1985)
3. Funeral by the Sea (New English Library 1982)
4. Three Graves to Showdown (New English Library 1982)
5. Back from the Dead (New English Library 1982)

338. THE VENGEANCE SEEKER
  By Will C. Knott
Wolf Caulder is the title character.
  The Vengeance Seeker (Ace 1975)
  The Vengeance Seeker No. 2 (Ace 1975)
  3. A Taste of Vengeance (Ace 1977)
  4. Caulder's Badge (Ace 1977)

339. THE VIGILANTE
  By Clint Reno
W.T. Ballard wrote these stories about Mark Doone, The Vigilante.
  1. Sun Mountain Slaughter (Fawcett 1974)
  2. Sierra Massacre (Fawcett 1974)

340. THE VIRGINIAN
  By Owen Wister and Dean Owen
Wister's influential novel spurred a television series, "The Virginian"
(1962-70), later called "The Men From Shiloh" (1970-71). The latter
prompted a paperback novel.
  The Virginian: A Horseman of the Plains by Owen Wister (Macmillan
1902)
  The Men from Shiloh: Trail for the Virginian by Dean Owen (Lancer
1971)

341. WACO
  By J.T. Edson
Another series from the British writer.
  Sagebrush Sleuth (Brown Watson 1962)
  Arizona Ranger (as Rod Denver) (Brown Watson 1962)
  The Drifter (Brown Watson 1963)
  Waco Rides In (Brown Watson 1964)
  Hound Dog Man (Brown Watson 1967)
  Doc Leroy, M.D. (Corgi 1977)
  Waco's Badge (Corgi 1981)

342. BIG JIM WADE
  By Luke Short
Frederick D. Glidden wrote as Luke Short. *Savage Range* first appeared
in a 1938 issue of *Western Story Magazine.*
  And the Wind Blows Free (Macmillan 1945)
  Savage Range (Dell 1980)

343. WAGONS WEST
  By Dana Fuller Ross
This saga series was instigated by Book Creations Inc.
  1. Independence! (Bantam)
  2. Nebraska! (Bantam 1979)
  3. Wyoming! (Bantam 1979)

4. Oregon! (Bantam 1980)
5. Texas! (Bantam 1980)
6. California! (Bantam 1981)
7. Colorado! (Bantam 1981)
8. Nevada! (Bantam)
9. Washington! (Bantam 1982)
10. Montana! (Bantam 1982)
11. Dakota! (Bantam 1983)
12. Utah! (Bantam 1984)
13. Idaho! (Bantam 1984)
14. Missouri! (Bantam 1984)
15. Mississippi! (Bantam 1985)
16. Louisiana! (Bantam 1986)

344. JOSEY WALES
By Forrest Carter
The first book was made into a 1976 movie with Clint Eastwood. It is about a former Confederate guerilla, hunted by the government, who choses to live in Indian territory. Reprinted in paper by Dell.
The Outlaw Josey Wales (Delacorte 1973)
The Vengeance Trail of Josey Wales (Delacorte 1976)

345. WAR CHIEF
By Edgar Rice Burroughs
The books are about an Indian warrior.
The War Chief (McCLurg 1927)
Apache Devil (Burroughs 1933)

346. WAR FOR THE UNION
By Everett T. Tomlinson
This is a boys' book series.
For the Stars and Stripes (Lothrop, Lee and Shepard 1909)
The Young Blockaders (Lothrop, Lee and Shepard 1910)

347. THE WARHUNTER
By Scott Siegel
Warfield Hunter is the title character
1. Killer's Council (Zebra 1981)
2. Gunmen's Grave (Zebra 1981)
3. The Great Salt Lake Massacre (Zebra 1981)
4. Bitter Blood (Zebra 1981)

348. WALT WARREN
By John Langley
Warren is a gun-carrying lawyer.
Six-Gun Trial (Hale 1958)
Six-Gun Feud (Hale 1959)
Six-Gun Law (Hale 1960)

Six-Gun War (Hale 1960)
Six-Gun Justice (Hale 1961)
Six-Gun Gamble (Hale 1963)
Six-Gun Strife (Hale 1963)
Six-Gun Champion (Hale 1964)
Six-Gun Citadel (Hale 1964)
Six-Gun Smoke (Hale 1965)
Six-Gun Cavalier (Hale 1965)
Six-Gun Vengeance (Hale 1966)
Six-Gun Salute (Gresham 1967)
The Badlands Gang (Hale 1970)

349. SAM WATCHMAN
By Brian Garfield
The hero is a contemporary Navajo police officer in this series reprinted by Fawcett.
Relentless (World 1972) (Hodder 1973)
Threepersons Hunt (Evans 1974) (Coronet 1975)

350. YOUNG WILD WEST
By An Old Scout
This series reprinted turn-of-the-century dime novels featuring Young Wild West in *Wild West Weekly*. The paperbacks also carried shorter stories about Denver Dan from *Wide Awake Library*. Listed are volumes known to have been issued; there may be more. The books are undated but appeared in the mid-1960s.
Young Wild West's Prairie Pioneers (Gold Star)
Young Wild West's Green Corn Dance (Gold Star)
Young Wild West and the Renegade Rustlers (Gold Star)
Young Wild West's Running the Gauntlet (Gold Star)
Young Wild West's Whirlwind Riders (Gold Star)
Young Wild West and the "Salted Mine" (Gold Star)

351. WESTERN INDIAN SERIES
By Elmer Russell Gregor
This is a boys' book series.
White Otter (D. Appleton 1917)
The War Trail (D. Appleton 1921)
Three Sioux Scouts (D. Appleton 1922)
The Medicine Buffalo (D. Appleton 1925)
The War Chief (D. Appleton 1927)
The Mystery Trail (D. Appleton 1927)

352. WESTERN QUINTET
By A.B. Guthrie
Guthrie's sweeping frontier adventure features Boone Caudill, a mountain man "driven by a raging hunger for life and a longing for the blue

sky and brown earth of the big, wild places."
The Big Sky (Sloane 1947) (Boardman 1947)
The Way West (Sloane 1949) (Boardman 1950)
These Thousand Hills (Houghton Mifflin 1956) (Hutchinson 1957)
Arfive (Houghton Mifflin 1971) (Eyre Methuen 1972)
The Last Valley (Houghton Mifflin 1975)

353. DICK WESTON
By Trygve Lund
The hero is a Mountie.
The Murder of Dave Bradan (Laurie 1931)
Weston of the Royal North West Mounted Police (Laurie 1928)
Weston of the North West Mounted Police (Mellifort 1938)
Robbery at Portage Bend (Kendall 1933)

354. WESTWARD RAILS
By Paul R. Rothweiler
Railroads are featured in this saga series.
Railroad King (Dell 1981)
Fortune's Mistress (Dell 1982)
Empire Builder (Dell 1982)

355. WHISKEY SMITH
By Eric Allen
Whiskey Smith is an untamed section of Indian Territory. The last two
books appeared in a double edition from Ace.
A Killer in Whiskey Smith (Ace)
Raiders from Whiskey Smith (Ace)
The Hanging at Whiskey Smith (Ace 1968)
Marshal from Whiskey Smith (Ace 1969)

356. THE WHISTLER
By E.B. Mann
Jim Sinclair is also known as The Whistler in these book by Edward
Beverly Mann.
Rustler's Roundup (Morrow 1935) (Collins 1936)
El Sombra (Morrow 1936) (Collins 1936)
The Whistler: Three Western Novelettes (Greenburg 1953) (Pocket
1954)

357. WHITE INDIAN
By Donald Clayton Porter
This saga series is about Renne, born to white parents but raised by
Seneca Indians during the colonial period. Later volumes carry on with
his son Ja-Gonh and his grandson GhonKaba. The series, put together by
Book Creations Inc., was first called the Colonization of America series.
1. White Indian (Bantam 1979)
2. The Renegade (Bantam 1980)

3. War Chief (Bantam 1980)
4. The Sachem (Bantam 1981)
5. Renno (Bantam 1981)
6. Tomahawk (Bantam)
7. War Cry (Bantam 1983)
8. Ambush (Bantam 1983)
9. Seneca (Bantam 1983)
10. Cherokee (Bantam 1984)
11. Choctaw (Bantam 1985)
12. Seminole (Bantam 1986)

358. WHITE SQUAW
By E.J. Hunter
Rebecca Caldwell is a half-breed raised by the Oglala in this adult series.
1. Sioux Wildfire (Zebra 1983)
2. Boomtown Bust (Zebra 1983)
3. Virgin Territory (Zebra 1984)
4. Hot Texas Tail (Zebra 1984)
5. Buckskin Bombshell (Zebra 1984)
6. Dakota Squeeze (Zebra 1984)
7. Abilene Tight Spot (Zebra 1984)
8. Horn of Plenty (Zebra 1985)
9. Twin Peaks — Or Bust (Zebra 1986)

359. WHITE WOLF
By Hal Dunning
The stories, which appeared in *Complete Stories* from 1928 to '34, are about Jim-Twin Allen, the White Wolf. Stories printed in *Wild West Weekly* 1938-43 were under the Dunning name but were written by Walker A. Tompkins and Paul S. Powers and weren't collected.
The Outlaw Sheriff (Chelsea House 1928)
White Wolf's Lair (Chelsea House 1928)
White Wolf's Pack (Chelsea House 1929)
White Wolf's Feud (Chelsea House 1930)
The Wolf Deputy (Chelsea House 1930)
White Wolf's Outlaw Legion (Chelsea House 1933)

360. WHITEWATER DYNASTY
By Helen Lee Poole
This saga series spotlights American rivers.
1. Hudson! (Zebra 1980)
2. The Ohio! (Zebra 1981)
3. Cumberland! (Zebra 1982)
4. The Wabash! (Zebra 1983)
5. Mississippi! (Zebra 1984)
6. The Missouri! (Zebra 1985)

361. HARRISON WIKLE
By Frank Roderus

The books are about an unlikely hero out to make a man of himself. The trilogy was reprinted in paper by Ballantine.
  Leaving Kansas (Doubleday 1983)
  Reaching Colorado (Doubleday 1984)
  Finding Nevada (Doubleday 1985)

362. WIND RIVER SERIES
  By Gary McCarthy
Struggles of two women in the pioneer west.
  Wind River (Ballantine 1984)
  Powder River (Ballantine 1985)

WINNING OF AMERICA
  See NARRATIVES OF AMERICA

363. WOLFEVILLE STORIES
  By Dan Quin
Alfred Henry Lewis wrote this series under a penname.
  Wolfville: Episodes of Cowboy Life (Stokes 1897) (Lawrence and Bullen 1897)
  Sandburrs (Stokes 1898)
  Wolfville Days (Stokes 1902) (Isbister 1902)
  Wolfville Nights (Stokes 1902) (Nelson 1924)
  Wolfville Folks (Stokes 1908)
  Faro Nell and Her Friends (Dillingham 1913)
  Old Wolfville: Chapters from the Fiction of Alfred Henry Lewis, edited by Louis Filler (Antioch Press 1968)
  Wolfville Yarns edited by Rolfe Humphries (Kent State University Press 1968)

364. WOMEN WHO WON THE WEST
  By Lee Davis Willoughby
Early entries in this saga series were designated as The Making of America Part 2 and were written under a house name later used extensively by the Making of America series (see that entry). Authors include Daniel Strieb.
  1. Tempest of Tombstone (Dell 1982)
  2. Dodge City Darling (Dell 1982)
  3. Duchess of Denver (Dell 1982)
  4. Lost Lady of Laramie (Dell 1982)
  5. Flame of Virginia City (Dell 1982)
  6. Angel of Hangtown (Dell 1982)
  7. Princess of Powder River (Dell 1982)

365. WOODRANGER TALES
  By George Waldo Browne
This is a frontier boys' book series.
  The Woodranger (L.C. Page 1899)

The Young Gunbearer (L.C. Page 1900)
The Hero of the Hills (L.C. Page 1901)
With Roger's Rangers (L.C. Page 1906)

366. X-BAR-X BOYS
By James Cody Ferris
This is a Stratemeyer Syndicate house name.
The X-Bar-X Boys on the Ranch (Grosset & Dunlap 1926)
The X-Bar-X Boys in Thunder Canyon (Grosset & Dunlap 1926)
The X-Bar-X Boys on Whirlpool River (Grosset & Dunlap 1926)
The X-Bar-X Boys on Big Bison Trail (Grosset & Dunlap 1927)
The X-Bar-X Boys at the Round-Up (Grosset & Dunlap 1927)
The X-Bar-X Boys at Nugget Camp (Grosset & Dunlap 1928)
The X-Bar-X Boys at Rustlers' Gap (Grosset & Dunlap 1929)
The X-Bar-X Boys at Grizzley Pass (Grosset & Dunlap 1929)
The X-Bar-X Boys Lost in the Rockies (Grosset & Dunlap 1930)
The X-Bar-X Boys Riding for Life (Grosset & Dunlap 1981)
The X-Bar-X Boys in Smoky Valley (Grosset & Dunlap 1932)
The X-Bar-X Boys at Copperhead Gulch (Grosset & Dunlap 1933)
The X-Bar-X Boys Branding the Wild Herd (Grosset & Dunlap 1934)
The X-Bar-X Boys at the Strange Rodeo (Grosset & Dunlap 1935)
The X-Bar-X Boys with the Secret Rangers (Grosset & Dunlap 1936)
The X-Bar-X Boys Hunting the Prize Mustangs (Grosset & Dunlap 1937)
The X-Bar-X Boys at Triangle Mine (Grosset & DUnlap 1938)
The X-Bar-X Boys and the Sagebrush Mystery (Grosset & Dunlap 1939)
The X-Bar-X Boys in the Haunted Gully (Grosset & Dunlap 1940)
The X-Bar-X Boys Seek the Lost Troopers (Grosset & Dunlap 1941)
The X-Bar-X Boys Following the Stampede (Grosset & Dunlap 1942)

367. YANKEE GIRL CIVIL WAR STORIES
By Alice Turner Curtis
This is a girls' book series.
A Yankee Girl at Fort Sumter (Penn 1920)
A Yankee Girl at Bull Run (Penn 1921)
A Yankee Girl at Shiloh (Penn 1922)
A Yankee Girl at Antietam (Penn 1923)
A Yankee Girl at Gettysbug (Penn 1924)
A Yankee Girl at Vicksburg (Penn 1926)
A Yankee Girl at Hampton Roads (Penn 1927)
A Yankee Girl at Lookout Mountain (Penn 1928)
A Yankee Girl at the Battle of the Wilderness (Penn 1929)
A Yankee Girl at Richmond (Penn 1930)

368. YAQUI
By Zane Grey and Romer Zane Grey
Zane Grey's warrior Yaqui from *Desert Gold* (originally serialized in

Popular Magazine) was reprised for short stories in *Zane Grey's Western Magazine* under the Romer Zane Grey house name. The Leisure volume also features a Burn Hudnall story based on the hero of Zane Grey's *The Thundering Herd* and Jim Cleve in another story following up his *The Border Legion* appearance. (That last novel was originally serialized in *All-Story.*)

    Desert Gold by Zane Grey (Harper 1913)
    The Thundering Hérds (Harper 1925)
    The Border Legion (Harper 1916)
    Zane Grey's Yaqui: Siege at Forlorn River by Romer Zane Grey (Leisure 1984) (Ian Henry 1986)

369. YOUNG KENTUCKIANS
    By Byron Archibald Dunn
This is a boys' book series about the Civil War.
    General Nelson's Scout (A.C. McClurg 1898)
    On General Thomas' Staff (A.C. McClurg 1899)
    Battling for Atlanta (A.C. McClurg 1900)
    From Atlanta to the Sea (A.C. McClurg 1901)
    Raiding with Morgan (A.C. McClurg 1903)

370. YOUNG MISSOURIANS
    By Byron Archibald Dunn
This is a boys' book series.
    With Lyon in Missouri (A.C. McClurg 1910)
    The Scout of Pea Ridge (A.C. McClurg 1911)
    The Courier of the Ozarks (A.C. McClurg 1912)
    Storming Vicksburg (A.C. McClurg 1913)
    The Last Raid (A.C. McClurg 1914)

371. YOUNG TRAILERS
    By Joseph A. Altsheler
This is a boys' book series.
    The Young Trailers (D. Appleton 1907)
    The Forest Runners (D. Appleton 1908)
    The Keepers of the Trail (D. Appleton 1916)
    The Eyes of the Woods (D. Appleton 1917)
    The Free Rangers (D. Appleton 1909)
    The Riflemen of the Ohio (D. Appleton 1910)
    The Scouts of the Valley (D. Appleton 1911)
    The Border Watch (D. Appleton 1912)

372. YOUNG VIRGINIANS SERIES
    By Byron Archibald Dunn
This is a boys' book series about the Civil War.
    1. The Boy Scouts of the Shenandoah (A.C. McClurg 1916)
    2. With the Army of the Potomac (A.C. McClurg 1917)
    3. Scouting for Sheridan (A.C. McClurg 1918)

373. WILSON YOUNG
By Giles Tippette
Young is a professional bank robber. The first book in the series was made into a film.
1. Bank Robber (Dell)
2. Wilson's Gold (Dell 1980)
3. Wilson's Luck (Dell 1980)
4. Wilson's Choice (Dell 1981)
5. Wilson's Revenge (Dell 1981)
6. Wilson's Woman (Dell 1982)
7. Hardluck Money (Dell 1982)
8. The Texas Bank Robbing Company (Dell)
9. Wilson Young on the Run (Dell 1983)

374. YUMA
By Russel Smith
Yuma is an Indian trying to survive in the white man's world.
Yuma (Leisure 1978)
Yuma: Renegade Gold (Leisure 1979)

375. ZORRO
By Various Authors
Senor Zorro (The Fox) is the Robin Hood of the Old West in stories first published in the pulps and hardcover. The hero was featured in a Walt Disney television program (1957-59) and movies. The first title was issued in paper by Dell.
The Mark of Zorro by Johnston McCulley (Grosset & Dunlap 1924) (MacDonald 1959)
The Further Adventures of Zorro by McCulley (Hutchinson 1926)
Zorro by Steve Frazee (Whitman 1958)
Zorro, the Gay Blade by Les Dean (Leisure 1981)
Zorro and the Pirate Raiders by D.J. Arneson (Bantam 1986)
Zorro Rides Again by Arneson (Bantam 1986)

ADDENDA
(Not Indexed)

29. BOLT
>   19. Palomino Stud (Zebra 1986)
>   20. Sixguns and Silk (Zebra 1986)

30. BONANZA
>   1. Winter Grass by Dean Owen (Popular Library 1968)
>   2. Ponderosa Kill by Owen (Popular Library 1968)

44. BUCHANAN
>   Buchanan's Stage Line (Fawcett 1986)

45. BUCKSKIN
>   11. Trigger Guard (Leisure 1986)
>   12. Recoil (Leisure 1986)

71. CIMARRON
>   21. Cimarron and the Manhunters by Kelley (Signet 1986)
>   22. Cimarron and the Hired Gun by Kelley (Signet 1986)

77A. ROOSTER COGBURN
>   Various authors
The books are about the crusty, one-eyed character played in two motion pictures by John Wayne.
>   True Grit by Charles Portis (Simon and Schuster 1966) (Cape 1967)
>   Rooster Cogburn by Martin Julien (New American Library 1975)

111. FLOATING OUTFIT
>   Master of Triggernometry (Corgi 1981) Trigger Master (Berkeley 1986)
>   Quest for Bowie's Blade (Berkley 1982)

121. FURY
>   Fury, Stallion of Broken Wheel Ranch (Holt, Rinehart & Winston 1959) (Tempo 1972)

132. GUNSMITH
>   54. Hell on Wheels (Ace Charter 1986)

55. The Legend Maker (Ace Charter 1986)
56. Walking Dead Man (Ace Charter 1986)

162. RUFF JUSTICE
    25. Jack of Diamonds (Signet 1986)
    26. Twisted Arrow (Signet 1986)

179. LASSITER
    4. Lassiter Tough by Loren Zane Grey (Pocket 1986)

193. LONE STAR
    46. Lone Star and the Mission War (Jove 1986)
    47. Lone Star and the Gunpowder Cure (Jove 1986)
    48. Lone Star and the Land Baron (Jove 1986)
    49. Lone Star and the Gulf Pirates (Jove 1986)

194. LONGARM
    90. Longarm in the Ruby Range Country (Jove 1986)
    91. Longarm and the Great Cattle Kill (Jove 1986)
    92. Longarm and Crooked Ranch (Jove 1986)
    93. Longarm on the Siwash Trail (Jove 1986)

195 LONGARM AND LONE STAR
    Longarm and the Lone Star Showdown (Jove 1986)

202A BAT MASTERSON
    Various authors
These books are based on the 1958-61 television
series featuring Gene Barry.
    Bat Masterson by Richard O'Connor (Bantam 1958)
    Bat Masterson by Wayne Lee (Whitman 1960)

206A DUDE McQUINT
    by Fred Grove
The series is about horse trader Dude McQuint and
his pards Coyote Walking and Uncle Billy Lockhart.
    The Great Horse Race (Doubleday 1977)
    Match Race (Doubleday 1982)
    Search for the Breed (Doubleday 1986)

246. RAIDER AND DOC
    60. The Northland Marauders (Berkley 1986)
    61. Blood in the Big Hatchets (Berkley 1986)
    62. The Gentleman Brawler (Berkley 1986)
    63. Murder on the Rails (Berkley 1986)

257. REEL WEST
   Third Reel West (Doubleday 1986)

258. RENEGADE
   34. The Golden Express (Warner 1986)
   35. Standoff in the Sky (Warner 1986)
   36. Guns for Garcia (Warner 1986)

262. RIN TIN TIN
   Rin Tin Tin and the Ghost Wagon Train by Cole
Fannin (Whitman 1958)

266A. RODEO
   By Red Mitchell
Jack "Doc" McDuff and Bob "Popcorn" Pruitt are
featured in this contemporary series about two rodeo
riders.
   1. Rodeo (Pinnacle)
   2. Slayride (Pinnacle 1982)

280. SCARLET RIDERS
   3. Beyond the Stone Heaps (Zebra 1986)

281. SCOUT
   20. Big Baja Bounty (Zebra 1986)
   21. Wildcat Widow (Zebra 1986)

282. SHELTER
   24. Tongue-Tied Texan (Zebra 1986)
   25. The Slave Queen (Zebra 1986)

282A. THE SHERIFF
   By D.R. Meredith
Crawford County Sheriff Charles Matthews is featured
in this contemporary crime series.
   The Sheriff and the Panhandle Murders (Avon)
   The Sheriff and the Branding Iron Murders (Avon
1986)

294. SLOCUM
   90. Cheyenne Bloodbath (Berkley 1986)
   91. The Blackmail Express (Berkley 1986)
   92. Slocum and the Silver Ranch Fight (Berkley
1986)

301. SPUR
   15. Hang Spur McCoy (Leisure 1986)

16. Rawhider's Woman (Leisure 1986)

303. STAGECOACH STATION
    23. El Paso (Bantam 1986)
    24. Mesa Verde (Bantam 1986)
    25. San Antonio (Bantam 1986)

317. SWEET MEDICINE'S PROPHECY
    5. Sun Dancer's Legacy (Zebra 1986)

331A. MATT TIERNEY
    By Tim Champlin
Matt Tierney is the hero of this paperback series.
    Summer of the Sioux (Ballantine 1982)
    Dakota Gold (Ballantine 1982)
    Staghorn (Ballantine 1984)

335. TRAILSMAN
    54. Killer Clan (Signet 1986)
    55. Thief River Showdown (Signet 1986)
    56. Guns of Hungry Horse (Signet 1986)

343. WAGONS WEST
    17. Tennessee! (Bantam 1986)

358. WHITE SQUAW
    10. Solid as a Rock (Zebra 1986)
    11. White-Headed Heathen (Zebra 1986)

360A. WHITEY
    By Glen Rounds
Whitey and his cousin Josie live on Uncle Torwal's
Rattlesnake Ranch in this hardcover juvenile series
illustrated by the author. The books have been
reprinted in paper.
    Whitey's First Roundup (Holiday House) (Avon
1982)
    Whitey Takes a Trip (Holiday House) (Avon 1982)
    Whitey and the Wild Horse (Holiday House)
    Whitey and the Colt-Killer (Holiday House 1962)
(Avon 1982)
    Whitey's New Saddle (Holiday House) (Avon 1982)

372. YAQUI
    Zane Grey's Yaqui and other Great Indian Stories
edited by Loren Grey (Belmont Tower 1976)

INDEX

Badlands Brigade, The (258)
Badlands Fury (15)
Badman's Bordello (29)
Badman's Range (141)
Badmen of Bordertown (141)
Badmen on Halfaday Creek (134)
Baja People, The (198)
Baker Street Breakout (177)
Bandido Blood (132)
Bandit Fury (281)
Bandit Gold (132) (294)
Bandit Queen, The (282)
Bandit Trail (43)
Bandit Trap, The (177)
Bandits in Blue (81)
Bandolero (109)
Bank Robber (373)
Bar B Boys, The or, The Young
  Cowpunchers (17)
Barbary Coast Tong (333)
Barbary Coasters, The (198)
Bar G Bunch, The (177)
Bar-20 (66)
Bar-20 Days (66)
Bar-20 Rides Again, The (66)
Bar-20 Three, The (66)
Bastard, The (21)
Battle Fury (310)
Battle of Blunder Ridge,
  The (177)
Battle of McAllister (203)
Battling for Atlanta (369)
Bawdy House Showdown (29)
Bayou Guns (141)
Beat the Drum Slowly (269)
Bedroll Beauty (131)
Beecher's Quest (177)
Before He Kills (177)
Beguinage (111)
Beguinage is Dead! (111)
Behind the Black Mask (224)
Behind the Swinging Doors
Believers, The (227)
Belle of the Rio Grande, The
  (185)
Bend of the River (177)
Best Man (11)
Betrayal (226)
Betty Zane (13)
Between Life and Death (164)
Beware the Smiling Stranger (52)
Beyond the Law (52)
Bibles, Bullets and Brides (246)
Big Country, Big Men (286)
Big Day at Blue Creek (177)
Big Dinero, The (177)
Big Drive, The (252)
Big Foot's Range (180)
Big Gamble, The (26)
Big Game, The (308)
Big Gold, The (104)
Big Gun, The (73)
Big Hunt, The (55)
Big Lobo (224)
Big Prize, The (309)
Big Sky, The (352)
Big Top Squaw (281)
Biggest Bounty, The (104)

Bill Hunter (150)
Bill Hunter's Romance (150)
Billy the Kid (146)
Birthright (61)
Bitter Blood (347)
Bitter Shield (312)
Black as Death (337)
Black Bulls, The (109)
Black Hat Riders, The (141)
Black Hawk's Warpath (157)
Black Hills Duel, The (85)
Black John of Halfaday Creek
  (134)
Black Pearl Saloon (132)
Black Rider, The (221)
Black Stallion Mesa (201)
Blackfoot Ambush (6)
Blackrobe (61)
Blacksnake Trail (242)
Blaine's Law (25)
Blaze (27)
Blaze of Guns, The (288)
Blazed Trail (229)
Blazing Guns (294)
Blessing Way, The (184)
Blind Side, The (104)
Blood at Sunset (302)
Blood Bait (145)
Blood Brother (11)
Blood Bullets (37)
Blood Cavalry (83)
Blood Chase (335)
Blood for a Dirty Dollar (200)
Blood Justice (131)
Blood Kin (144)
Blood Knife (180) (314)
Blood Line (11)
Blood Mesa (282)
Blood Money (31) (144)
Blood Moon (325)
Blood Oath (335)
Blood of Kings (283)
Blood of the Conquerors (276)
Blood of the North (99)
Blood on McAlister (203)
Blood on Silver (104)
Blood on the Border (138) (258)
Blood on the Hills (310)
Blood on the Moon (162)
Blood on the Prairie (314)
Blood on the Tracks (11)
Blood on the Yukon Trail (99)
Blood Rising (11)
Blood River (177)
Blood Run (104)
Blood Runner (258)
Blood, Sweat and Gold (246)
Blood Trail (138)
Blood Wedding (11)
Bloodbrothers (61)
Bloody Border (308)
Bloody Border, The (73)
Bloody Christmas (54)
Bloody Earth (164)
Bloody Gold (307)
Bloody Heritage (335)
Bloody Sands (246)
Bloody Shiloh (326)

Hot as a Pistol (274)
Hot Lead and Cold Nerve (288)
Hot Lead Trail (75)
Hot Sky Over Paraiso, (177)
Hot Texas (358)
Hound Dog Man (341)
Hour Before Disaster, The (224)
Hour of Jeopardy (177)
House on the Range (104)
Hudson! (359)
Hungry Gun, The (54)
Hunt Angel (10)
Hunt the Beast Down (299)
Hunt the Man Down (85)
Hunted Gun (40)
Hunters, The (314)
Hunters of the Hills, The (114)
Huntsville Breakout (333)

Idaho! (343)
Idaho Raiders (264)
In Kentucky with Daniel Boone (46)
In Memory of Marty Malone (177)
In Texas with Davy Crockett (46)
In the Great Wild North (156)
In the Heart of Texas (246)
In the Ranks of Old Hickory (334)
In the Rockies (46)
In Those Days (276)
In Tragic Life (151)
Incident at Horcado City (244)
Incident in a Texas Town (52)
Independence! (343)
Indian Incident, The (24)
Indian Maid (301)
Indian Outpost (264)
Indian Silver (157)
Inheritors (61)
Injun and Whitey (35)
Injun and Whitey Strike out for
  Themselves (35)
Injun and Whitey to the Rescue
  (35)
Inside Straight (26)
Into Mexico with General Scott
  (334)
Intrigue on Halfaday Creek (134)
Iron Horse Country (209)
Iron-Horse Gunsmoke (201)
Iron Men (314)
Iron Mustang (294)
Iroquois Scout, The (156)
It Happend on Halfaday Creek (134)

J. T.'s Ladies (55)
Jackson Hole Trouble (294)
Jailbreak Moon (294)
Jed McLane and the Storm Cloud
  (206)
Jed McLane and the Stranger (206)
Jed Smith, Freedom River (4)
Jenner Guns, The (306)
Jim Bridger, Mountain Man (4)
Jim Mason, Backwoodsman (202)
Jim Mason, Scout (202)
John Bozeman, Mountain Journey (4)
John Fremont, California Bound (4)

John Slaughter's Way (291)
Johnny Nelson (66)
Johnny Osage (227)
Jokers Wild (177)
Jory (161)
Joseph Walker, Frontier Sheriff (4)
Journey of Death, The (294)
Jubal Sackett (272)
Judas Horse, The (16)
Judas Killer, The (335)
Judas Tree, The (305)
Judge Colt (165)
Judgement at Poisoned Well (96)
Judgement Day (182)
Jury of Six (305)
Justice at Spanish Flat (286)
Justice for Jenner (224)
Justice of Company Z, The (112)
Justice on Halfaday Creek (134)

Kamakazi Justice (287)
Kanata (312)
Kane (163)
Kane and the Goldbar Killers (163)
Kane and the Outlaw's Double
  Cross (163)
Kansan's Lady, The (165)
Kansan's Woman (165)
Kansas Hex (177)
Kansas Kitten (131)
Kansas Marshal (264)
Kansas Trail (15)
Keep Allison Alive (177)
Keepers of the Trail, The (371)
Ken and the Cattle Thieves (166)
Ken Bails Out (166)
Ken Follows the Chuck Wagon (166)
Ken Hits the Cowboy Trail (166)
Ken in Alaska (166)
Ken on the Argentine (166)
Ken on the Navajo Trail (166)
Ken Range Dective (166)
Ken Rides the Range (166)
Ken Saddles Up (166)
Ken South of the Border (166)
Kentuckians, The (227)
Kentucky Spitfire--Caitlyn (119)
Kid Breckinridge (40)
Kid Daybreak (224)
Kid Light Fingers (177)
Kid Wichita (224)
Kid with a Colt (15)
Kilburn (170)
Kill Angel (10)
Kill Dusty Fog! (73)
Kill McAllister (203)
Killer Bait (224)
Killer Caravan (335)
Killer Country (142)
Killer Grizzley (132)
Killer in Whiskey Smith, A (355)
Killer Lion (30)
Killer Mountains, The (308)
Killer Silver (54)
Killers, The (65)
Killers Breed (104)
Killers Came at Noon (224)
Killer's Council (347)

Lone Ranger on Powderhorn Trail, (191)
Lone Ranger on the Red Butte Trail (191)
Lone Ranger Rides, The (191)
Lone Ranger Rides Again, The (191)
Lone Ranger Rides North, The (191)
Lone Ranger Traps the Smugglers, The (191)
Lone Ranger West of Maverick Pass (191)
Lone Ranger's New Deputy (191)
Lone Star and the Alaskan Guns (193)
Lone Star and the Amarillo Rifles (193)
Lone Star and the Apache Revenge (193)
Lone Star and the Apache Warrior (193)
Lone Star and the Badlands War (193)
Lone Star and the Biggest Gun in the West (193)
Lone Star and the Border Bandits (193)
Lone Star and the Buffalo Hunters (193)
Lone Star and the California Oil War (193)
Lone Star and the Denver Madam (193)
Lone Star and the Devil's Trail (193)
Lone Star and the Ghost Pirates (193)
Lone Star and the Gold Mine War (193)
Lone Star and the Gold Raiders (193)
Lone Star and the Golden Mesa (193)
Lone Star and the Hangrope Heritage (193)
Lone Star and the Hardrock Payoff (193)
Lone Star and the Kansas Wolves (193)
Lone Star and the Land Grabbers (193)
Lone Star and the Mescalero Outlaws (193)
Lone Star and the Mexican Standoff (193)
Lone Star and the Montana Troubles (193)
Lone Star and the Moon Trail (193)
Lone Star and the Mountain Man (193)
Lone Star and the Opium Rustlers (193)
Lone Star and the Oregon Trail (193)
Lone Star and the Owlhoot Trail (193)
Lone Star and the Railroad War (193)

Lone Star and the Renegade Comanches (193)
Lone Star and the Rio Grande Bandits (193)
Lone Star and the Riverboat Gambler (193)
Lone Star and the San Antonio Rais (193)
Lone Star and the School for Outlaws (193)
Lone Star and the Showdowners (193)
Lone Star and the Stockyard Showdown (193)
Lone Star and the Texas Gambler (193)
Lone Star and the Timberland Terror (193)
Lone Star and the Tombstone Gamble (193)
Lone Star and the Utah Kid (193)
Lone Star and the White River Curse (193)
Lone Star Bodyguards (177)
Lone Star Firebrands (177)
Lone Star Fury (177)
Lone Star Godfathers (177)
Lone Star Hellions (177)
Lone Star in the Cherokee Strip (193)
Lone Star in the Tall Timber (193)
Lone Star Lucky (177)
Lone Star Massacre, The (246)
Lone Star on Outlaw Mountain (193)
Lone Star on the Treachery Trail (193)
Lone Star on the Treasure River (193)
Lone Star Peril (141)
Lone Star Ranger (100)
Lone Star Reckless (177)
Lone Star Reckoning (177)
Lone Star Rider (288)
Lone Star Rowdy (177)
Lone-Star Stud (29)
Lone Star Valiant (177)
Lone Star Vengeance (177)
Lone Trail for Cheyenne (159)
Loner, The (104)
Lonely Men, The (272)
Lonely on the Mountain (272)
Long, Hard Ride (165)
Long Winter (187)
Longarm (194)
Longarm and Santa Anna's Gold (194)
Longarm and the Avenging Angels (194)
Longarm and the Bandit Queen (194)
Longarm and the Big Outfit (194)
Longarm and the Big Shootout (194)
Longarm and the Blackfoot Guns (194)
Longarm and the Blindman's

Waiting For a Train (104)
Waiting Game, The (54)
Walk Tall, Ride Tall (62)
Wanderer of the Wasteland (176)
Wanted for Murder (308)
Wanted: Wildcat O'Shea (231)
Wanted Woman (282)
War Chief (357)
War Chief, The (345) (351)
War Clouds (82)
War Cry (357)
War Dance at Red Canyon (177)
War Devils (325)
War Eagle, The (102)
War in the Painted Buttes (242)
War on Charity Ross (268)
War Party (314)
War Trail (314)
War Trail, The (351)
Warm Flesh and Hot Lead (165)
Warn Angel (10)
Warpaint (158)
Warpaint and Rifles (335)
Warpath (226)
Warrior Range (201)
Warriors, The (20) (21)
Warriors of the Code (198)
Warrior's Path, The (272)
Washington! (343)
Washington's Young Scouts (7)
Watch Out for Wildcat (231)
Waxahachie Smith (295)
Way of the Tiger, the Sign of the
  Dragon, The (174)
Way of the Wind, The (155)
Way West, The (352)
Wayward Kind, The (177)
We Are Betrayed (151)
Weapon Heavy (147)
Wear Black for Johnny (224)
Wear the Star Proudly (224)
We're From Texas (177)
Wes Hardin's Gun (147)
West of Omaha (158)
West of Railhead (129)
West of the Pecos (141)
Weston of the North West Mounted
  Police (353)
Weston of the Royal North West
  Mounted Police (353)
Whalers, The (198)
What Crime is It? (197)
Wheels of Thunder (128)
Wheels Out of Jericho (177)
When Legends Die (235)
When Legends Meet (132)
When Santiago Fell or, The War
  Adventures of Two Chums (115)
Whip and the War Lance, The (55)
Whiplash (237) (244)
Whiskey Guns (335)
Whistler, The: Three Western
  Novelettes (356)
White Gold of Texas (141)
White Hell (294)
White Hell Trail, The (335)
White Indian (111) (357)
White Otter (351)

White Savage (335)
White Stallion, Red Mare (55)
White Wolf, The (102)
White Wolf's Feud (360)
White Wolf's Lair (360)
White Wolf's Outlaw Legion (360)
White Wolf's Pack (360)
Who Killed Rice? (177)
Wichita (303)
Wichita Gunman (282)
Widow Creek (162)
Widow Maker, The (131)
Wild and the Wayward, The (198)
Wild Bill's Ghost (132)
Wild Dancer, The (198)
Wild Horse Lightning (242)
Wild Horse Shorty (283)
Wild Horse Valley (84)
Wild Hunt, The (76)
Wild Stallions, The (314)
Wild Trail to Denver (177)
Wild, Wild Women (274)
Wildcat Against the House (231)
Wildcat Meets Miss Melody (231)
Wildcat on the Loose (231)
Wildcat Roundup (132)
Wildcat Takes His Medicine (231)
Wildcat Woman (274)
Wildcats, The (111)
Wildcat's Claim to Fame (231)
Wildcat's Rampage (231)
Wildcat's Revenge (231)
Wildcat's Witch Hunt (231)
Wildcatters, The (109) (198)
Wilderness Empire (222)
Wilderness Seekers (198)
Wilderness War, The (222)
Wildfires (312)
Willing Target, The (224)
Wilson Young on the Run (373)
Wilson's Choice (373)
Wilson's Gold (373)
Wilson's Luck (373)
Wilson's Revenge (373)
Wilson's Woman (373)
Wind Power (362)
Windwolf (162)
Wings of the Hawk (275)
Winners and Losers (177)
Winnetou (228)
Winnetou's Heritage (228)
Winning Hand, The (333)
Winslow Freight (192)
Winter Adventures of Three Boys
  in Great Lone Land (328)
Winter Drift (25)
Winter Hell (131)
Winter's Love (317)
With Boone on the Frontier, or
  the Pioneer Boys of Old
  Kentucky (115)
With Carson and Fremont (334)
With Custer in the Black Hills or,
  A Young Scout Among the
  Indians (115)
With Flintlock and Fife (80)
With George Washington Into
  the West (334)